FS
100

FOR KING & EMPIRE

OTHER CANADIAN BATTLEFIELDS OF THE GREAT WAR

Festubert, May 1915
Givenchy, June 1915
Hill 70 & Lens, August 1917

A Social History and Battlefield Tour

by

Norm Christie

FOR KING & EMPIRE; VOLUME II - REVISED

CEF BOOKS
2007

Library and Archives Canada Cataloguing in Publ
Christie, Norm M.,
Other Canadian battlefields of the G
Givenchy, and Hill 70 / Norman M. Christie.
(For king & empire ; v. 9)
ISBN 978-1-896979-19-9
1. World War, 1914-1918–Campaigns–France.
History —World War, 1914-1918. 3. World W
France– Guidebooks. I. Title. II. Other Canadia
1916-17.
D528.C48 2007 940.4'144

Published by: CEF BOOKS
P.O. Box 40083
Ottawa, Ontario, Canada, K1V 0W8.
1-613-823-7000
www.cefbooks.ca

Other books in this Series

Volume I:	*The Canadians at Ypres, 22-26 April 1915 (Revised)*
Volume II:	*The Canadians on the Somme, Sept.-Nov. 1916 (Revised)*
Volume III:	*The Canadians at Vimy, April 1917 (Revised)*
Volume IV:	*The Canadians at Passchendaele, Oct.-Nov. 1917 (Revised)*
Volume V:	*The Canadians at Arras, August-September 1918 (Revised)*
Volume VI:	*The Canadians at Cambrai, September-October 1918 (Revised)*
Volume VII:	*The Canadians at Amiens, August 1918*
Volume VIII:	*The Canadians at Mount Sorrel, June, 1916*
Volume IX:	*Other Canadian Battlefields of the Great War*
Volume X:	*The Newfoundlanders in the Great War, 1916-18*

The publisher would like to thank Sheila Hanratty of Ottawa, and Dave and Linda Horton of Manotick, Ontario.

Front cover: The view of the slagheaps of the Douai Plain from Petit Vimy British Cemetery. (PHOTO: N .Christie).

Printed in Canada

This book is dedicated
to the memory of my good friends,

John and Hazelle Laffin

THESE DEEDS
WHICH SHOULD NOT PASS AWAY
NAMES THAT MUST NOT WITHER

On the Western Front, 1915.

TABLE OF CONTENTS

The Smile of Victory.

Introduction

This book is about three of Canada's lesser known battles of the First World War. The three battles varied significantly in scope and outcome, but they have in common thread that they have been forgotten. Today no Canadian Monuments mark the battlefields. They were abandoned, left to return to being farmers' fields or village streets. Sadly there is nothing to remind us about what took place 90 years ago. Yet 3,500 Canadians died on those cratered fields and in the ruined villages in the Battles of Festubert, Givenchy, and Hill 70.

The three battles were very different. Festubert and Givenchy were fought in 1915 in the soggy soil of French Flanders, and like so many First World War battles, were indecisive and costly. Hill 70 was a major operation which utilized three Canadian Infantry Divisions, artillery and engineers, and was a brilliant, limited-objective success. Each battle offered its contribution to the development of the Canadian Corps and helped it reach its spectacular efficiency by the summer of 1918.

The Battle of Festubert, May 15th-25th, 1915, was one of a series of battles fought by the British Army in 1915 (the others were Neuve Chapelle and Aubers Ridge) to assist the French Offensives north of Arras. It was Canada's first big action after losing 6,000 men in the Second Battle of Ypres. The newly-replenished Canadian battalions had a supporting role to the main British and Indian assaults. After the first days of fighting they were ordered to attack over difficult terrain in the face of superior German machine-gun and artillery fire. Remarkably they managed to move the line forward and achieve what was asked of them at the cost of 2,500 casualties.

Givenchy took place three weeks later and was a small localized action (officially called an "Action", it was not big enough to be termed a "Battle"), fought three km south of Festubert. It was a limited strike, involving only a few British and Canadian battalions, which was a good thing as the balance of fire at this time was so much to the German advantage that the attackers had little chance. The Canadians involved in the fighting did manage to break into the German line, but could not hold on. They did add a Battle Honour and a posthumous Victoria Cross at the cost of 600 men.

The Battle of Hill 70 is in complete contrast to the others. It took place after the capture of Vimy Ridge, when the Canadians were in peak form. Their Generals were tried and capable and the men confident. It was a localized battle, intended to bite off an important piece of the German line and then punish the Germans when they counter-attacked. They succeeded in taking the German line, and advanced into the suburbs of Lens. Often the Canadians had to fight house-to-house and basement-to-basement in the ruins of the city. The operation was well-planned and well-executed, but still claimed 9,194 casualties, including 2,400 Canadian lives. It is an indication of the intensity of the fighting that six Victoria Crosses were won by the Canadians in the battle. Three were posthumous.

In the 1920s when Canada was considering which Battles to commemorate Festubert, Givenchy and Hill 70 were not considered significant enough to rate one of the eight Canadian Battle Monuments. So today there is nothing to remind us of what took place. There is little evidence of war at these places. A quick eye can find a concrete pillbox or two and there are the ever-present cemeteries. The cemeteries truly hold the secrets of these battles. The Maple Leaf on each headstone creates a link with Home and reminds us of the Canadians who died here.

It is the objective of this book to act as a memorial to the men who fought in these battles. It is only appropriate we should honour the sacrifices of the Canadians who died at Festubert, Givenchy and Hill 70, and remember these lost battlefields.

About Arras

To be consistent with other guides in this series Arras has been recommended as your centre of operations for visiting these Canadian Battlefields. However there is also excellent accommodation in Bethune and Lille. Ieper (Ypres) in Belgium is also an excellent base, being only 60 km from Festubert and 80 km from Hill 70 and Lens.

Arras is the capital of the Artois region of northern France. Historically it has been the scene of many wars and the objective of many invading armies. This was the case during the First World War when the Germans briefly overran the city in 1914, and were driven out after a brief occupation. Arras was never far from the frontline and throughout the next four years was constantly bombarded. Its beautiful architecture was badly damaged by the shell-fire and it gained the reputation of being a "martyred" place, much like Ypres. Virtually every Canadian who fought in the war knew Arras. It is in many ways, one of those soulful cities that was deeply imbued in the consciousness of the Great War generation.

It is the perfect place to visit the First World War battlefields. The Somme is only 30 km south, Cambrai is 30 km east and even Ypres is only 100 km north.

Arras has been witness to much warfare over the centuries. Of Roman origin, it was a stronghold in Julius Caesar's day. It was originally called Atrebatum after a tribe which lived in the area, the Atrebates. Arras is a corruption of that name.

Arras became part of the kingdom in France in the mid-17th century, prior to that it successively belonged to the Counts of Flanders (850-1180), to the Counts of Artois (1180-1384), to the Dukes of Burgundy (1384-1492) and finally to the Kings of Spain (1492-1640). Birth place of Augustin Robespierre, Arras was not spared during the Revolution. In 1793, Joseph Le Bon, sent there on a mission, organized the Terror. The guillotine was permanently erected in the Place de la Comédie.

During the Great War, the Germans occupied Arras for only three days, September 6th-9th, 1914. But after their departure, the "Martyrdom of Arras" began. Bombardment began October 6th, 1914. Gunners fired ceaselessly on the city. The Hôtel de Ville, the Abbey of Saint Vaast and the Cathedral were burnt down, the Befroi (belfry) destroyed and by April 1917, Arras was completely in ruins. In March 1918, when

Getting There

This guide recommends Arras as the centre of operations for visiting the battlefields. Arras is located in the Pas-de-Calais and is easily accessible from Paris (170 km) and Brussels (120 km). From London, it is a two-hour drive to Dover, a 75 minute ferry ride to Calais, and a 90 minute drive from Calais. The opening of the Channel Tunnel has made a direct rail link from London to Lille, France, which is 45 minutes from Arras. Rental cars are available in any of the above-mentioned cities and tourist offices can supply routes and details of hotels.

In Arras very little English is spoken so brush up on your French before you leave. Most stores close between noon and 2 p.m., always be sure to get all your necessities before lunch!

The Euro has replaced the French (and Belgian) Franc. The current exchange rate for Euros is roughly 1.50 Canadian dollars per Euro (2007). Always visit the Tourism Office to obtain information on accommodation and events of interest.

Theft is a real problem in France (car break-ins in particular). The local thieves will smash your windows or drill the lock, take what they want and be gone in seconds. Do not leave anything in plain view in your car and try to leave your vehicle within sight if possible. You have been warned.

The French are always ‘upgrading’ their road systems, so it suggested you use an up-to-date road map with this book.

What To Bring

Weather is very changeable in this part of Europe. For example, the average temperature in Belgium in July varies from 12 to 24°C. Days can start sunny and change quickly to rain, hail or even a sprinkling of snow. Above all, be prepared for wet weather.

Other than the obvious, a passport, traveller’s checks and appropriate clothing, bring the following to ensure a successful trip:

-a bottle opener and cork screw
-binoculars
-a camera
-a compass
-rubber boots
-Michelin map 236 (Use in conjunction with the new CWGC booklet available at the CWGC Office at Beaurains)
- IGN maps 2404E and 2405E (available at stores in Arras)
-a journal to record the details of your visit, because you will forget.

the great German Offensive began, the bombardments broke out anew, and the inhabitants were evacuated. But the City did not fall. In August, 1918 the Canadians drove the enemy beyond Arras for good.

During the Second World War Arras was captured by the Germans in May 1940. There was some fighting just south of Arras when British Armour gained a brief victory over Erwin Rommel's marauding Panzers. There is a Royal Tank Corps Memorial opposite the Town Hall in Beaurains commemorating this action. The Nazis ruled Arras with an iron fist. A grim reminder of the German oppression is the Mur des Fusilles (behind the Citadel). This is where 218 French resistants and hostages were executed by the Germans. It is a spooky place and well worth a visit. Arras was finally liberated by the British Army in September 1944.

A visit to Arras should begin in the architecturally-unique Grand'Place, once an orchard belonging to the Abbey of Saint Vaast, and the Petite-Place. These squares have been bordered with gabled private houses and edged with stone columns and elliptical arches supporting vaulted galleries for hundreds of years.

Bordering the west side of the Petite-Place is the Hôtel de Ville, above which rises the graceful silhouette of the belfry. Long the centre of town, the Petite-Place attracted the townspeople to public meetings, festivals and public executions.

Today, the tourist office is located at the Hôtel de Ville (03 21 51 26 95) and is open daily. From there, guided tours can be arranged of the underground tunnels (souterrains) beneath the town hall (35 minutes, year-round).

Accommodation is not a problem in Arras. You may want to check out the following hotels:

Astoria, 10 place Foch, 62000 Arras, tel. 03 21 71 08 14
Hôtel Ibis, place Viviani, 62000 Arras, tel. 03 21 23 61 61
Hôtel Moderne, 1 boulevard Faidherbe, tel.03 21 23 39 57

The Canadian Expeditionary Force, 1915-1917

1ST CANADIAN DIVISION

(Festubert - 1915, Givenchy -1915, Hill 70 - 1917)

1ST INFANTRY BRIGADE	2ND INFANTRY BRIGADE	3RD INFANTRY BRIGADE
1ST BATTALION (WESTERN ONTARIO)	5TH BATTALION (SASKATCHEWAN)	13TH BATTALION (THE BLACK WATCH)
2ND BATTALION (EASTERN ONTARIO)	7TH BATTALION (BRITISH COLUMBIA)	14TH BATTALION (ROYAL MONTREAL REGIMENT)
3RD BATTALION (TORONTO REGIMENT)	8TH BATTALION (90TH RIFLES OF WINNIPEG)	15TH BATTALION (48TH HIGHLANDERS)
4TH BATTALION (CENTRAL ONTARIO)	10TH BATTALION (ALBERTA)	16TH BATTALION (CANADIAN SCOTTISH)

2ND CANADIAN DIVISION

(Hill 70 - 1917)

4TH INFANTRY BRIGADE	5TH INFANTRY BRIGADE	6TH INFANTRY BRIGADE
18TH BATTALION (WESTERN ONTARIO)	22ND BATTALION (QUEBEC)	27TH BATTALION (CITY OF WINNIPEG)
19TH BATTALION (CENTRAL ONTARIO)	24TH BATTALION (VICTORIA RIFLES OF MONTREAL)	28TH BATTALION (SASKATCHEWAN)
20TH BATTALION (CENTRAL ONTARIO)	25TH BATTALION (NOVA SCOTIA)	29TH BATTALION (BRITISH COLUMBIA)
21ST BATTALION (EASTERN ONTARIO)	26TH BATTALION (NEW BRUNSWICK)	31ST BATTALION (ALBERTA)

3RD CANADIAN DIVISION

7TH INFANTRY BRIGADE	8TH INFANTRY BRIGADE	9TH INFANTRY BRIGADE
ROYAL CANADIAN REGIMENT (NOVA SCOTIA)	1ST MOUNTED RIFLES (SASKATCHEWAN)	43RD BATTALION (CAMERON HIGHLANDERS)
PRINCESS PATRICIA'S CANADIAN LIGHT INFANTRY (EASTERN ONTARIO)	2ND MOUNTED RIFLES (BRIT. COLUMBIA)	52ND BATTALION (NEW ONTARIO)
42ND BATTALION (BLACK WATCH OF MONTREAL)	4TH MOUNTED RIFLES (CENTRAL ONTARIO)	58TH BATTALION (CENTRAL ONTARIO)
49TH BATTALION (ALBERTA)	5TH MOUNTED RIFLES (QUEBEC)	116TH BATTALION (ONTARIO COUNTY)

4TH CANADIAN DIVISION
(Hill 70 - 1917)

10TH INFANTRY BRIGADE	11TH INFANTRY BRIGADE	12TH INFANTRY BRIGADE
44TH BATTALION (MANITOBA)	54TH BATTALION (BRITISH COLUMBIA)	38TH BATTALION (EASTERN ONTARIO)
46TH BATTALION (SASKATCHEWAN)	75TH BATTALION (MISSISSAUGA HORSE)	72ND BATTALION (SEAFORTHS)
47TH BATTALION (BRITISH COLUMBIA)	87TH BATTALION (GRENADIER GUARDS OF MONTREAL)	78TH BATTALION (WINNIPEG GRENADIERS)
50TH BATTALION (ALBERTA)	102ND BATTALION (NORTH BRITISH COLUMBIANS)	85TH BATTALION (NOVA SCOTIA HIGHLANDERS)

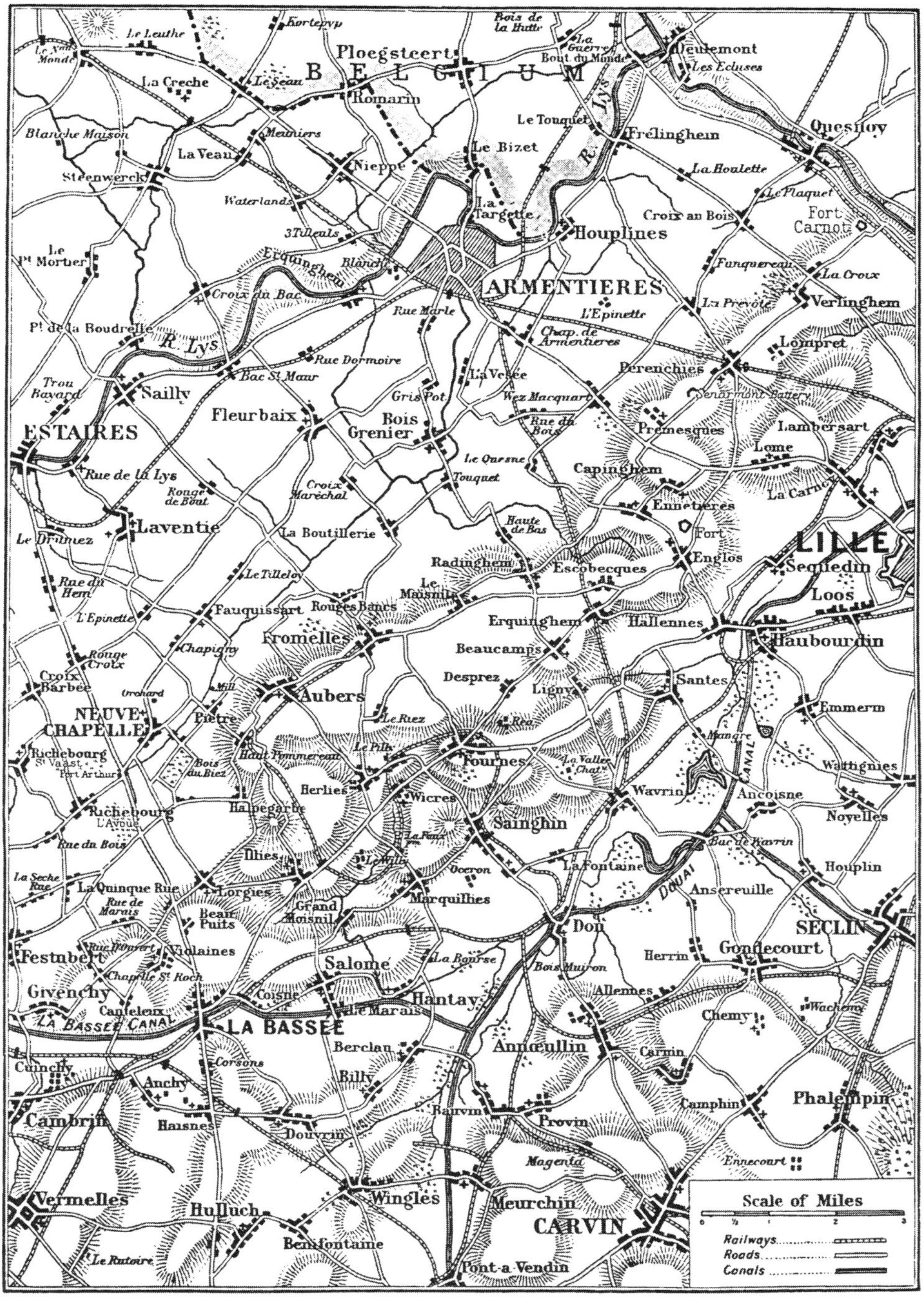

Map of the battle front between Armentieres and La Bassee showing the fortified horse-shoe ridge which formed so formidable a barrier to the British attack on the German entrenchments before Lille.

Historical Overview

The Battle of Festubert, May 15th-25th, 1915
The Second Action of Givenchy, June 15th-16th, 1915

By the winter of 1914-1915 the war had settled into a stalemate. After the Race to the Sea, both sides had dug in and a line of trenches now extended from the English Channel to the Swiss border. The Germans held most of Belgium and a large area of Northern France. The French were impatiently awaiting their first opportunity to drive the Germans back and were ready to take the offensive in the spring of 1915. They put pressure on the British to assist in their upcoming attacks and although short of men and munitions, the British agreed.

The British Army was small in 1914 and they had suffered terrible casualties in the great battles of Mons and The Aisne. Britain had been mobilising, but did not have enough trained troops to be truly ready to take the offensive. In late 1914 the Indian Corps of two divisions, and the first British Territorial (militia) units had arrived in France. British industry was still gearing up to produce the required guns and shells. Regardless of his limited resources Sir John French, the British commander, committed his divisions to attack a German position centred on the village of Neuve Chapelle.

At this point in the war the Generals had little experience fighting a modern enemy in entrenched positions, supported by great quantities of machine-guns and artillery. Neuve Chapelle was to be the first test for the British Army.

The 1st Canadian Division Arrives

The 1st Canadian Division had been training on the Salisbury Plain since October 1914. Finally in early February, 1915 the 20,000 men of the Division had embarked for France and were immediately moved to the front at Fleurbaix to get their first exposure to trench warfare. It was during this period that the 1st Division suffered their first casualties, primarily through sniping. By March 10th, 1915 the Canadians were holding four km of the front north of Neuve Chapelle. The main attack was to be a British/Indian assault on the German trenches at Neuve Chapelle, five km south. The Canadians were asked to provide a diversion, which

Major Actions in the La Bassee Canal to Armentieres Sector, 1914-18

The Battle of La Bassee, October 10th - November 2nd, 1914 On October 10th-13th newly arrived British and Indian troops drove back the Germans towards Lille, stabilizing the line between Armentieres and Aubers Ridge. On October 20th, 1914 the Germans counter-attacked and recaptured Aubers Ridge, and Neuve Chapelle. The British retained their line east of Armentieres. The British and Indians suffered 20,000 Casualties.

Minor actions: Defence of Festubert, November 23rd-24th, 1914, when the Indian Army repelled German attacks. Defence of Givenchy, December 20th-21st, 1914, when the Indian Army repelled German attacks.

The Battle of Neuve Chapelle, March 10th-13th, 1915 British and Indian troops pushed the Germans out of Neuve Chapelle, and gained 2,000 yards. Commonwealth casualties were 12,000.

The Battle of Aubers Ridge, May 9th, 1915 In an effort to assist French offensives at Arras, the British launched a two-pronged attack on Aubers Ridge. One attack is launched at Nueve Chapelle and the other against Fromelles. The attacks failed, and is called off after one day. 11,000 British and Indian casualties.

The Battle of Festubert, May 15th-25th, 1915 British, Indian and Canadian troops launch an attack towards Aubers Ridge, to assist the French attacking north of Arras. Minor gains. Total commonwealth casualties, 17,000.

The Battle of Fromelles, July 19th, 1916 An attack intended to divert German reserves from the Battle of the Somme. Australian and British troops try to break through to Fromelles, but are decimated in their attempt. Total Australian and British casualties, 7,000.

The Battle of the Lys, April 9th-29th, 1918 Major German offensive launched April 9th, 1918. Seven Divisions hit Portugese, and breakthrough. They advance 8 km, but Festubert and Givenchy hold. On April 10th, 1918, the Germans attack from Armentieres to Ypres with great success, but within days British, Australian and French reinforcements slow the advance. On April 30th, the German offensive, which reached points east of Hazebrouck and Bethune, is called off. Commonwealth losses number 78,000 men.

just meant that they would fire their rifles and machine-guns over the parapet to get the enemy's attention.

The Battle of Neuve Chapelle, March 10th-13th, 1915

On March 10th, after a 35 minute bombardment, four British and Indian Divisions launched their attack on the German positions on a three km front. Initially the attack went well, but in the face of heavy artillery fire and German counter-attacks the advance stalled. After three days of fighting the British/Indian force had advanced two km and suffered almost 12,000 casualties. The attack had failed to breakthrough the Germans; but it was felt that with more artillery and troops, that the next time it would work. Plans for further operations were quickly put in place, but before the British could resume the fighting the Germans launched their gas attack at Ypres.

The Canadians at Ypres

The 1st Canadian Division had been moved from the Fleurbaix sector in mid-April to the Ypres Salient. On the afternoon of April 22nd the Germans released chlorine gas on French Colonial troops holding the northern sector of the Salient. In their first real battle the Canadians fought to stem the German advance and over the next four days succeeded in doing so at a cost of 6,000 killed, wounded and prisoners. It was a terrible yet courageous action by the inexperienced Canadians, who faced the gas, but whose gallant defence saved the situation. (See *The Canadians at Ypres, April 22nd-26th, 1915*; For King & Empire; Vol I; CEF Books, Revised 2005.)

On May 3rd, 1915 the Canadians were pulled out of the line at Ypres and the depleted battalions were reinforced by 4,000 new men. Within two weeks they were back in the line, south of Armentieres. They would be given a supporting role in the upcoming Battle of Festubert.

The Battle of Aubers Ridge, May 9th, 1915

During the time the Canadian Division was being reformed, the British Army had launched another attack to assist the French, who were fighting a desperate battle with the Germans north of Arras, at Neuville-St. Vaast, Notre Dame de Lorette and Vimy Ridge.

The Battle of Aubers Ridge was fought on May 9th on a 14 km front (from north of Festubert to Fromelles). The original plan had been to coordinate the British and French attacks. The British would provide a northern pincer that would seize the German positions on Aubers Ridge.

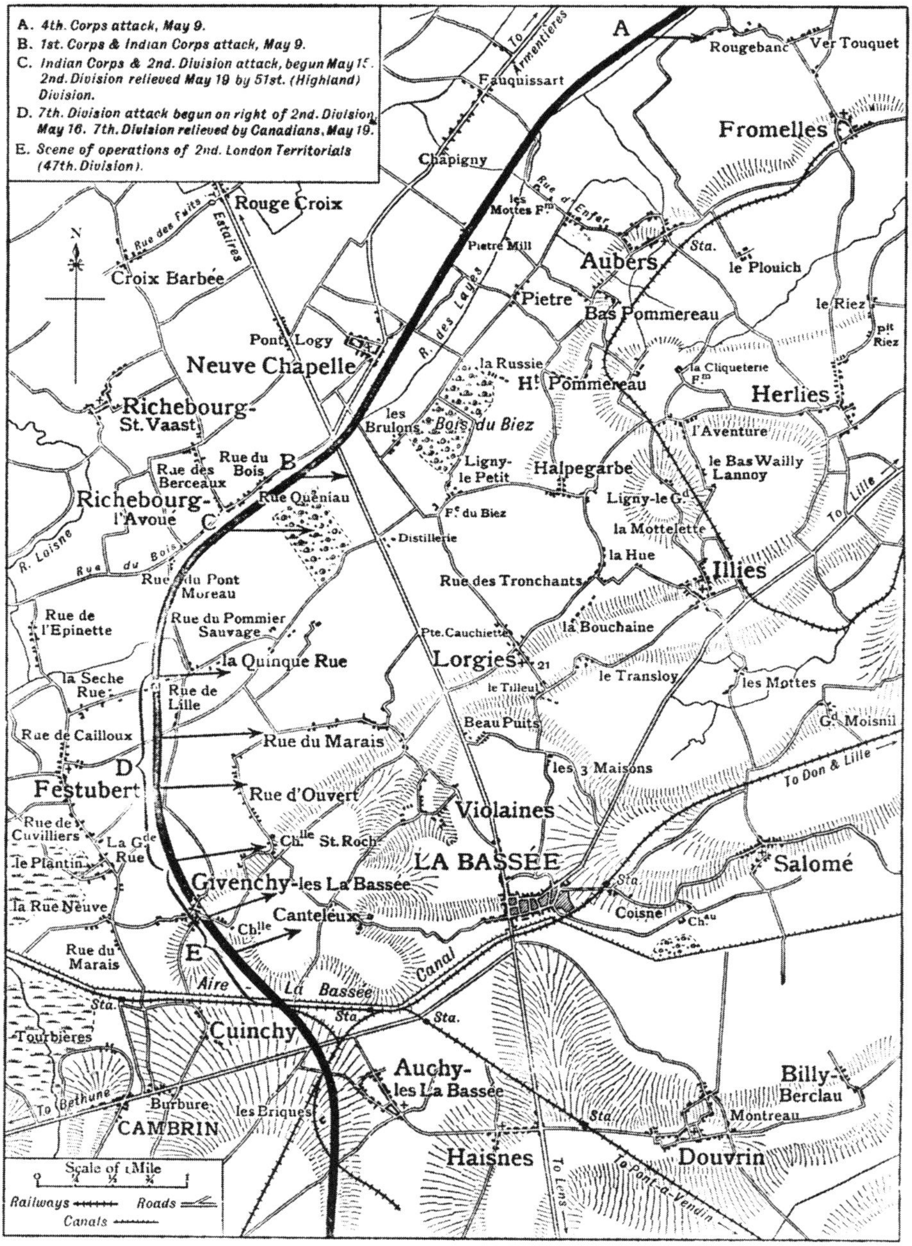

Map illustrating the Operation of the First Army, under Sir Douglas Haig, during May and June, 1915.

The Capture of the German Trenches at Neuve Chapelle.

The Ridge was considered the major obstacle protecting the German-occupied city of Lille. The French, simultaneously, would take Vimy Ridge and threaten the Germans from the south.

Six British and Indian Divisions were employed in the attack that began at 5:40 am on May 9th. The attack was an abject failure with few troops getting through the wire and fewer still entering the German trenches. Most were shot down as they crossed No Man's Land. The lack of artillery was unable to destroy the German positions or even cut the barbed wire in many places. In less than 12 hours the battle had to be called off, but in that time the attackers had lost 11,000 men.

However the British command still felt obliged to do what they could for the French and decided to resume the offensive a few days later near the village of Festubert. This time the Canadians would be a part of the attacking force.

The Battle of Festubert, May 15th-25th, 1915

Festubert was a continuation of the other British battles in 1915. Its purpose was to assist the French, even though British manpower and munitions were limited.

The German trenches at Festubert were all built above ground, sand-bag breastworks, two or three sandbags deep and 6-8 feet tall. The ground in this area was water-logged so the digging of proper trenches was not possible. The land is flat with no distinctive landmarks, which would be a problem in keeping the orientation of an attack. In addition wide ditches, 3-4 metres across, filled with water, cut through the area. The enemy incorporated these moats into their defensive positions. The Germans also held the distinctive advantage of controlling Aubers Ridge, from where all Allied movement could be observed, and severely punished by their artillery.

Northeast of Festubert the German positions consisted of a redoubt, known as the Quadrilateral, a fortified farm (Ferme du Bois), and a series of breastworks, the two largest being the North and South Breastwork. The Breastworks contained strong-points and acted as effective communication trenches.

The plan was to attack from two directions. At 11:30 pm on May 15th British and Indian troops would advance one km south from the Rue du Bois. Four hours later other troops would attack from the west, jumping off from the main line, one km NE of Festubert village.

British troops at the Front in Flanders, 1915. The sandbag breastworks were used by both sides. In this area the water table was so high regular trenches could not be dug.

The initial assault in the darkness was unable to breakthrough the German line. Only in one place did the attackers enter the enemy line. The second attack was more successful, the men left their trenches at 3:45 am on May 16th, and drove back the Germans 500 yards, capturing the front line, and in some places pushing beyond. But the Germans were still putting up a dogged defence at the Quadrilateral. On May 17th the northern part of the attack was halted and the main thrust was now to come from the Festubert Sector. The British troops captured the Quadrilateral, but the Germans had reacted quickly to the British advance and had dug a new defensive line from Ferme du Bois to the South Breastworks. Douglas Haig, the Commander of the First Army, saw this as the "enemy's resistance breaking down," and changed the Battle's objectives to the capture of La Bassee, 8 km away.

Haig called up his reserves, including the 3rd Canadian Infantry Brigade and the Guards, and ordered an attack on the afternoon of May 18th. But due to confused communications his orders for a 4:30 pm attack were not received by the Canadians until 3:20. They did not arrive on their jump-off position until 5:20, by which time the Guards had already attacked, and been shot down by the Germans. The Canadian attack went in late, but the 14th (Royal Montreal Regiment) and the 16th (Canadian Scottish) Battalions did advance. The 14th moved the line ahead by 400 metres north of La Quinque Rue, and the 16th got into the North Breastwork. They continued the fight into the 19th.

In the meantime the rest of the 1st Canadian Division relieved the British troops on the battlefield.

On May 20th the 16th and 15th (48th Highlanders of Toronto) Battalions attacked again, this time the 16th took the Orchard, and the 15th completed the capture of the North Breastwork.

The 2nd Canadian Brigade, commanded by Arthur Currie, was to attack SE of Festubert and capture part of the South Breastwork, and in particular a Strong-point known as K.5 (Bexhill). Currie personally reconnoitred the battlefield and discovered the maps he had were inaccurate, and without any distinguishable landmarks, he could not determine where the sand-bag feature, K.5, was. The area was a maze of old and new trenches, with sand-bags and bodies strewn about. He asked for a postponement, but his request was denied. The 10th Battalion (Alberta) attacked, and was shot down as it crossed No Man's Land.

On the 21st, Currie's men once again attacked the South Breastwork.

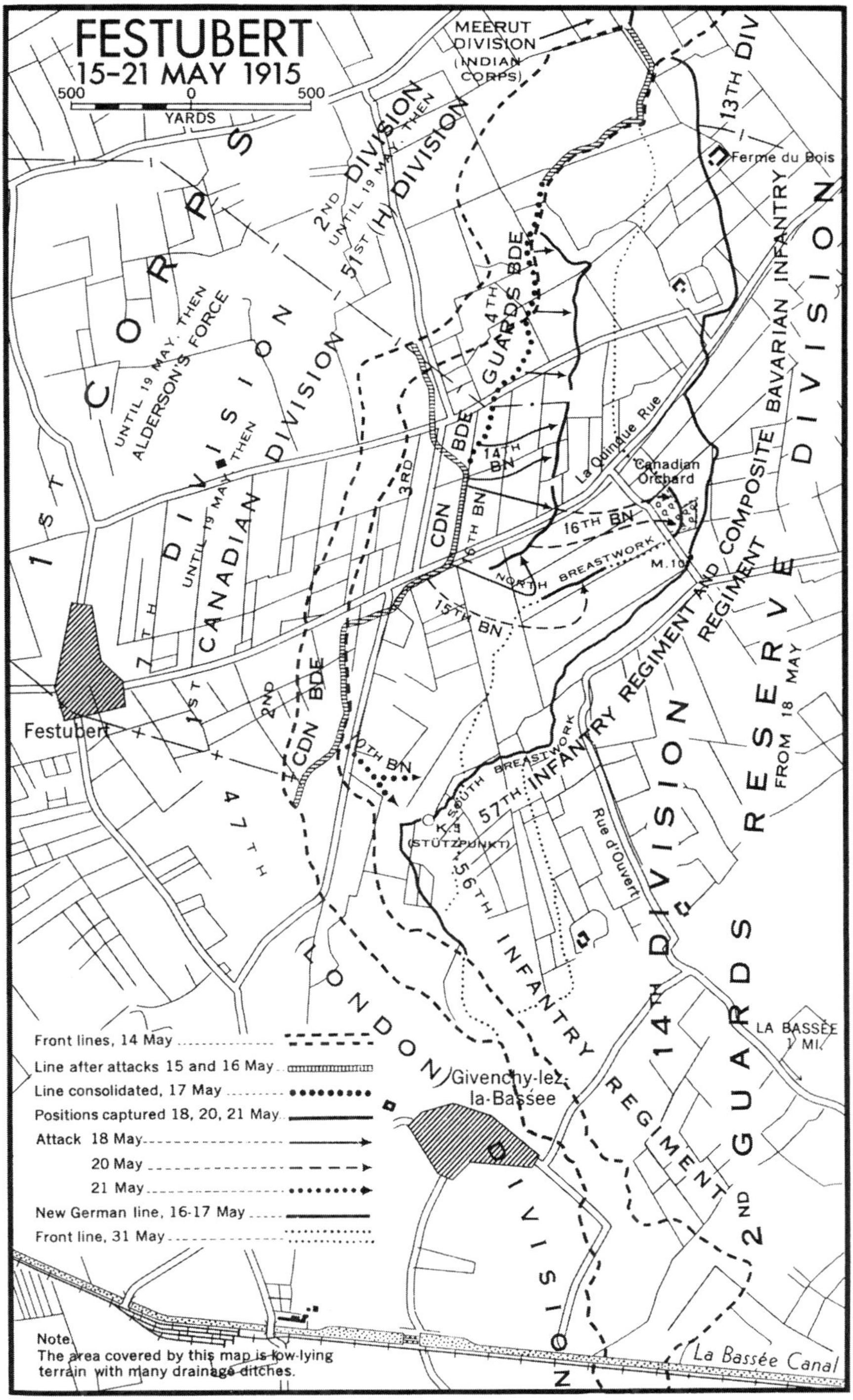
FESTUBERT
15–21 MAY 1915
500 0 500
YARDS
1ST CORPS
1ST CANADIAN DIVISION
UNTIL 19 MAY, THEN ALDERSON'S FORCE
7TH DIVISION UNTIL 19 MAY, THEN CANADIAN DIVISION
2ND DIVISION UNTIL 19 MAY, THEN 51ST (H) DIVISION
MEERUT DIVISION (INDIAN CORPS)
13TH DIV
Ferme du Bois
4TH GUARDS BDE
3RD CDN BDE
14TH BN
16TH BN
15TH BN
La Quinque Rue
Canadian Orchard
NORTH BREASTWORK
M.10
2ND CDN BDE
1ST
Festubert
47TH
LONDON DIVISION
SOUTH BREASTWORK
K.5 (STÜTZPUNKT)
57TH INFANTRY REGIMENT
56TH INFANTRY REGIMENT
INFANTRY REGIMENT AND COMPOSITE REGIMENT
BAVARIAN INFANTRY DIVISION
RESERVE DIVISION FROM 18 MAY
14TH DIVISION
2ND GUARDS RESERVE DIVISION
Rue d'Ouvert
LA BASSÉE 1 MI.
Givenchy-lez-la-Bassée
La Bassée Canal
Front lines, 14 May
Line after attacks 15 and 16 May
Line consolidated, 17 May
Positions captured 18, 20, 21 May
Attack 18 May
20 May
21 May
New German line, 16-17 May
Front line, 31 May
Note
The area covered by this map is low-lying terrain with many drainage ditches.

Tenaille, Major Daniel Jean, 5th Battalion, C.E.F., son of Alexandre Tenaille, of Paris Magistrate; born Paris, 16 Jan. 1880; educated Lycee, Chambery, Savoy, France; went to Canada, became Major 27th Light Horse, 1910; retired 1912 to go to the West Indies, but on outbreak of war rejoined the C.E.F., went overseas on Oct. 1914; to France Feb. 1915, and was killed in action at Festubert 24 May 1915; buried Le Touret Military Cemetery, II. C. 13. Colonel A.C. McDonald wrote, "Your son had taken several courses with me in Winnipeg, where I was commandant of the Cavalry School, and commanded Lord Strathcona's Horse... He was extremely popular with all ranks of the Strathcona's, and deservedly so. Personally, I looked upon him as a dear friend and a fine officer of the best type. On the early morning of 24 May, two companies of his regiment were ordered to assault a small German redoubt that was about 200 yards to our front; this was done with the greatest dash and gallantry, and amongst those splendid soldiers all were agreed that no one did better or displayed more courage than your son, he was easily 'le plus brave des braves'; the attack was met by a storm of shrapnel and machine-gun fire, and word passed to me that the supports of the 5th Battn. had not arrived, and that they required supports. Strathcona's were then holding the trenches on the right of our brigade; I threw in C Squadron. Our men told me that as they charged they passed Major Tenaille wounded on the ground, but he raised himself and cheered them - an incident that will always be remembered in the regiment that will cherish his memory. He must have died soon after that, and we trust he did not suffer much pain. When I saw him myself, he was lying on the ground about half way to the redoubt, on the south side of the German communication trench. Will you accept the deepest sympathy of all ranks of the Strathcona's Horse in your great sorrow. His brother wrote, "Daniel left the trenches the Sunday morning. In the night he had the order to return there with his men to take a trench in front of the place where he had been the previous days. At two in the morning he gave the signal of assault. It was done splendidly. Germans then concentrated a terrible fire on the piece of ground conquered from them and made a counter-attack. A bullet reached him at the hip. His company was already terrifically decimated, and he took hold of a machine-gun whose servants had all been killed, and served at it more than an hour. The German counter-attack was then pushed back, but supports were required. He went 100 yards behind to look for them. He found other officers, and sat down beside them because of the pain in his leg. A shrapnel shell hit them - all were wounded, Daniel was killed." Married in Corsica, Diane, 1905; and had four children; Charles, 1905; Andre, 1909; Georges, 1910, and Marie Anita, 1907.

This time after a two hour barrage the men of the 10th and 5th (Saskatchewan) Battalions raced across No Man's Land, and captured 400 metres of the enemy line. The Germans turned their heavy guns on them, and finally forced them to retire.

Dissatisfied with the advance Haig removed the Canadian Commander, Edwin Alderson, and took control of the battle himself. He wanted to renew the attack on May 24th. This time men of the 1st Canadian Brigade, the 3rd Battalion (Toronto) would attack east from the Orchard, now known as Canadian Orchard, into the German lines. The 2nd Brigade would go after K.5 once again.

When the attack was launched some men of the 3rd did break into the German line, but they were cut-off and killed or taken prisoner. As the 3rd Battalion attacked from the Orchard, the 5th and 7th (British Columbia) Battalions launched a determined assault on the South Breastwork, and finally after 30 minutes of fighting K.5 was in their hands. In the fighting for K.5 the 10th Battalion suffered 268 casualties and the 5th Battalion, 250.

The next day dismounted Canadian Cavalry of the Lord Strathcona's Horse, made an attempt to take a bit more of the South Breastwork, but were unable to push the line forward.

Finally on May 25th, 1915 the Battle of Festubert was called off. For a gain of two km the British Army had lost 14,500 men, killed, wounded and missing. Canadian losses were 2,468, including 661 dead.

Festubert left a lasting impression on 2nd Brigade Commander, Arthur Currie, " This was my first difference with the High Command. I protested on the grounds of insufficient time for reconnaissance and preparation. I now know better than ever I was right, but I was ordered to make the attack." Currie went on, " We were given two jobs to do, and did them. Since, I received the message, 'Well done, 2nd Brigade', but while some messages are deeply appreciated, they do not console. There I lost 53 officers and 1,200 men."

The Canadians would meet one of the architects of the Festubert disaster later on the Somme. As Commander of the Reserve (5th) Army Hubert Gough would order attacks against uncut barbed wire without proper preparations, with terrible results. Currie must have soured on Gough at Festubert and the Somme, for at Passchendaele in 1917, Currie refused to serve under him. Haig, the Commander of the British Expeditionary Force, allowed Currie his way, and reorganized the Armies to accommodate Currie's wishes.

The confusion of the British operation at Festubert was characteristic of all the French Flanders battles of 1915. In every battle the objectives chosen were too ambitious and there was never enough artillery. Poor communication resulted in lost opportunities, and there was generally poor leadership. These failures led to unnecessary losses. In addition, German superiority in artillery, tactics and communication would trump every Allied attack in 1915.

The Second Action of Givenchy, June 15th-16th, 1915

The Battle of Givenchy (or the Second Action of Givenchy as it is officially known) was the dying remnant of all the British plans to capture Aubers Ridge and assist the French. It typifies the mind set of the Generals, in that they could not comprehend that their strategies for breaking the German line would not work. The Action of Givenchy is the tail-end of the offensive that had started at Neuve Chapelle and had been unsuccessfully continued at Aubers Ridge and Festubert. An attack was planned over a limited front from Givenchy in the south to Festubert in the north.

For Givenchy the Generals had scaled down their ambitions and numbers of soldiers. They would commit to the attack only three Divisions, all worn-out from the earlier battles. In fact only 7 Battalions, including one Canadian, were designated for the attack. How or why the Generals thought this could possibly succeed is not known.

In June 1915 the Canadians had been shifted two km south to the Givenchy Sector. They were given the line from Givenchy to the La Bassee Canal.

In the upcoming attack one Canadian battalion, the 1st (Western Ontario) covering the right flank, would attack. The Canadians had learned from the Festubert disaster that to succeed they must neutralize the forward German machine-guns. To do this they moved three 18 pounder guns into the front lines. Two of the guns were only 75 metres from the enemy front line. The plan was for them to fire over open sites at the enemy strong-points. In addition a mine would be blown under the German line just before zero hour, and it was hoped their charge across No Man's Land would be covered in the confusion that followed.

Over two days British artillery fired a slow bombardment on the German lines, with the intensity increasing in the last 12 hours before zero. At 5:45 pm on June 15th, 1915 the two Canadian 18 pounders

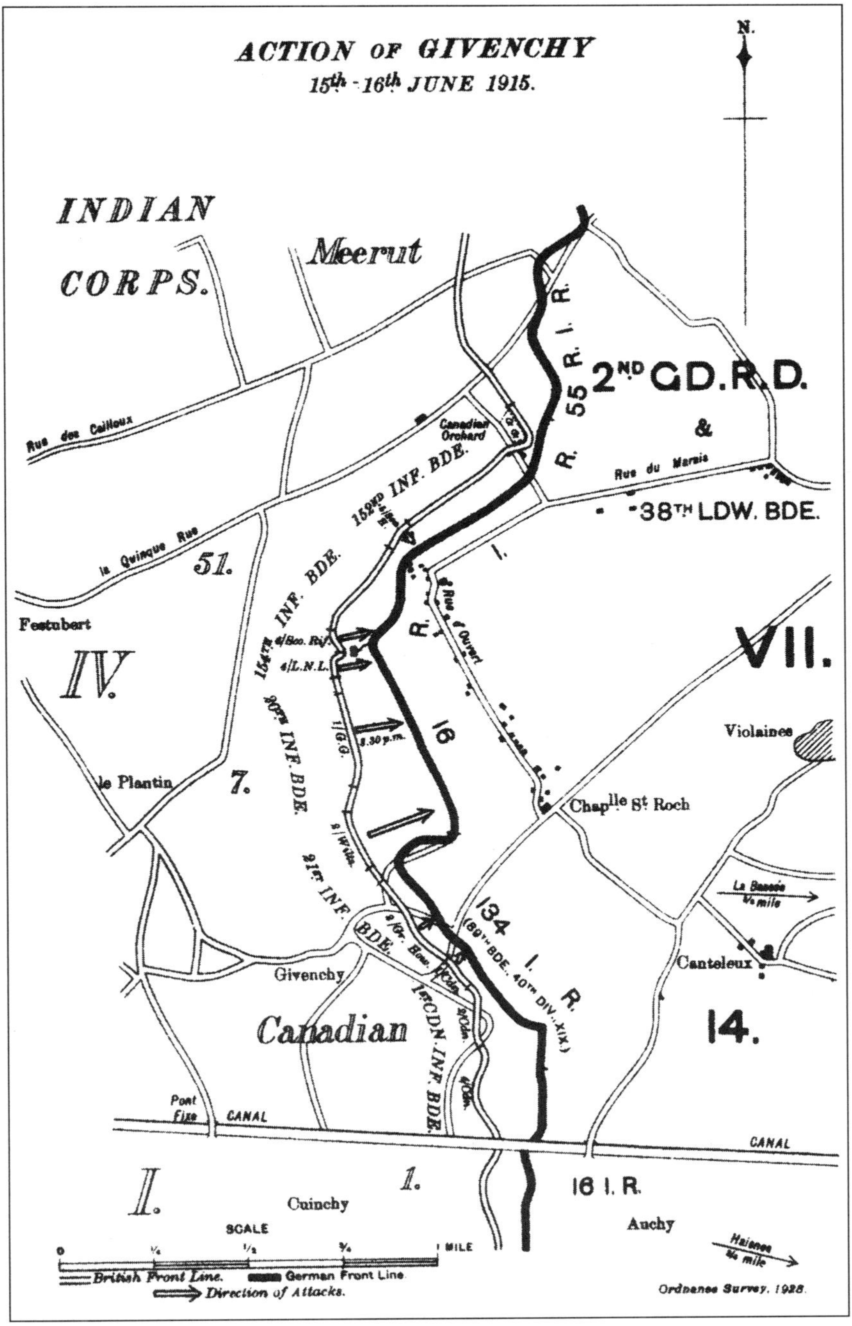
ACTION OF GIVENCHY
15th - 16th JUNE 1915.
N.
INDIAN
CORPS.
Meerut
2ND GD.R.D.
&
38TH LDW. BDE.
55 R. I. R.
Rue des Cailloux
Canadian Orchard
152ND INF. BDE.
Rue du Marais
la Quinque Rue
51.
154TH INF. BDE.
Festubert
IV.
VII.
4/L.N.L.
1/G.G.
20TH INF. BDE.
16
Violaines
le Plantin
7.
Chaplle St Roch
21ST INF. BDE.
La Bassée
Canteleux
134 I. R.
Givenchy
Canadian
1ST CDN. INF. BDE.
14.
Pont Fixe
CANAL
CANAL
I.
1.
Cuinchy
16 I. R.
Auchy
SCALE
0
1/4
1/2
3/4
1 MILE
British Front Line.
German Front Line.
Direction of Attacks.
Ordnance Survey, 1928.

opened up on the German line, and 13 minutes later the mine went up. Unfortunately it was short of the German line and inflicted casualties on the bombers of the 1st Battalion. At 6:00 pm the Canadians stormed across No Man's Land, and captured the German Strong-point H.3 (also known as Stony Mountain) in 10 minutes. Some men tried to clear the front line by bombing down the trench, while a second group broke into the German second line, 200 metres on.

In the second line they ran into heavy opposition, and with the British attacks on their flanks failing, the men from London, Ontario were on their own. Heavy German machine-gun fire traversed No Man's Land making it nearly impossible for reinforcements to cross. The men were now isolated, and German counter-attacks were forming up and bombers were closing in on the Canadians.

Lieutenant Campbell, machine-gun officer of the 1st Battalion, took his Vickers across to help cover any retirement. After most of the crew was killed and the gun damaged, Campbell, already wounded, and Private Howard Vincent were determined to drive the Germans back. Campbell put the broken Vickers on Vincent's back and fired 1,000 rounds at the attacking Germans. Campbell's bravery saved the lives of many men, who were desperately trying to get back to the Canadian lines. For this action Campbell was awarded the Victoria Cross and Vincent, of Bracebridge, Ontario, the Distinguished Conduct Medal. Amazingly Vincent escaped unscathed with the damaged Vickers. Unfortunately Frederick Campbell, VC, died of his wounds four days later at Boulogne. *(Frederick William Campbell; born Mount Forest, Ontario, June 15th, 1867; died June 19th, 1915; buried Boulogne Eastern Cemetery, II.A.24.)*

Men of the 2nd and 3rd Battalions tried to help the withdrawal by securing the mine crater, and this was of great assistance. By 11 pm June 15th, 1915 the Canadians had pulled back to their own lines. During the day the 1st Battalion had suffered 386 casualties, 46% of their entire strength.

All along the line the attack failed so it must have been a surprise when orders were received to remount the attack the next day. On June 16th, 1915 the 3rd Battalion was given the job of attacking. After a two hour bombardment, at 4:45 pm they attacked. They could not get into the German line before they were shot down. A soldier watching the attack observed, " The attack seemed, and seems, from every angle one

Lieutenant Campbell and Private Vincent hold off the Germans, June 15th, 1915.

Taking of K.5

"'Bexhill' proper, however, had to be taken, and to that end the two companies of the 5th Battalion, which were in reality inadequate to capture so strong a position, were reinforced by a company from the 7th Battalion and a squadron of Strathcona's Horse. With this reinforcement the attack was immediately pressed home, and 'Bexhill' and 130 yards of trenches towards the north fell into our hands at 5.49 a.m."

Greenwood, Lance Corporal Robert; 1st Battalion, C.E.F.; eldest son of Robert Greenwood of Camberwell, England; born Leytonstone, England, 25 Jan. 1895; went to Canada in Feb. 1914, and settled at Thamesford, Ontario, and worked as a farmer's helper; volunteered on the outbreak of war, and went overseas in Oct. 1914, and to France in Feb. 1915, and was killed in action at Givenchy 15 June 1915, being blown to pieces by a shell; unmarried. Commemorated on the Vimy Memorial.

Helliwell, Captain Joseph Grant, 1st Battalion, C.E.F.; 2nd son of Grant and Anna Helliwell of Toronto; born Toronto, 26 Nov. 1888; educated at the University of Toronto (Applied Science, 1910); served in the Essex Militia; enlisted on the outbreak of war; went overseas Oct. 1914; to France Feb. 1915; and was killed in action at Givenchy, 15 June 1915; unmarried. Lieut. Brian Henderson wrote, "At Givenchy the 1st Battn. did the attack. His company and D. Coy were to start the attack. Our artillery had been shelling the German trench and had made a very good job of cutting the wire. On Tuesday, June 15, the artillery opened up a terrific bombardment of the German trench and kept this up for three hours when at 5:58 pm a mine was blown up. One minute later those two companies went over our parapet and in a few seconds had arrived at the German trench which contained only a lot of dead; but machine guns on the flank were working; also the German artillery was doing terrific damage and the men began to fall in large numbers. At this trench Capt. Wilkinson was hit, and Joe took over the company and led them to the next trench. An officer who saw him leading his men said it was magnificent, especially as he thought Joe had already been hit in the arm. He got as far as the next trench, but was seen to fall with a bullet through his head. The trenches taken had to be given up as the supporting divisions were unable to get on, and it was impossible to stay out with both flanks unprotected."

viewed it, as futile and hopeless... The attackers had no supporting fire. They were mostly shot down as they climbed over the parapet. None of them got over 25 yards, except, perhaps, a few who were trapped in the sap and could do nothing but lie low and await a chance to return."

The 3rd Battalion lost 115 men, killed and wounded, at Givenchy. Total Canadian losses for two days fighting were 802, including 300 killed. British losses for the Second Action of Givenchy totalled 3,009.

Finally on June 19th the fighting was called off and the Canadians moved north to take up a new sector of the line at Ploegsteert Wood. Since the 1st Canadian Division arrived at the Front at the end of February 1915, they had fought in two major battles, and lost 9,500 men. In four months of war more than 3,400 Canadians had died.

The Duck's Bill Crater, looking towards La Bassee. The scene of the attack by the First Canadian Infantry Battalion, June, 1915.

Historical Overview

The Battle of Hill 70, August 15th-25th, 1917

The Battle of Hill 70 was one of the finest actions fought by the Canadian Corps in the Great War. It was a well-planned and finely executed operation. It was designed to bite off an strategic chunk of the German defences protecting the coal mining region around Lens. Hill 70 was also the first operation the Corps fought under their new commander, Lieutenant General Sir Arthur Currie. In June 1917 Currie had taken over from General Sir Julian Byng who had been promoted to command the Third British Army. Arthur Currie was a Canadian-born Militia officer who had commanded the 2nd Brigade at Ypres in 1915 and rose to lead the 1st Canadian Division to a few spectacular victories in 1916-17. He was not a particularly lovable man, but his thorough planning and openness to ideas not his own more than compensated for any personal weaknesses. He was also devoted to the Corps and would risk his career to object to any plans that were not in his men's interests. Hill 70 was one of these occasions.

The Canadians of 1917 were not the men of 1915. The Canadian Corps was now four Divisions, 100,000 men. In 1917 they had won great victories at Vimy Ridge, Arleux and Fresnoy. Julian Byng, the Canadian Corps Commander from May 1916, had moulded the Canadians into a fine fighting formation, known for efficiency and success. When Currie succeeded Byng as Commander of the Corps, he continued on with the work Byng had started and by the summer of 1917 the Canadians had a swagger that only comes from winning.

The British Army had successfully opened its Flanders Offensive against the Messines Ridge in June 1917. The next phase of operations, in what became known as Third Battle of Ypres or Passchendaele, would commence on July 31st, 1917. The Canadians were asked to provide a diversionary attack, to draw off enemy troops by capturing the coal-mining town of Lens. The area bordering the town was flooded and dominated by German positions amidst the slag heaps and ruins. Currie's men knew the area well, having fought there since May 1917. Against such defences any attack would meet disaster and Currie knew it, so he voiced his dissent and proposed an alternative, Hill 70, north of Lens. As an indication of the esteem held for Currie and the Canadians, the

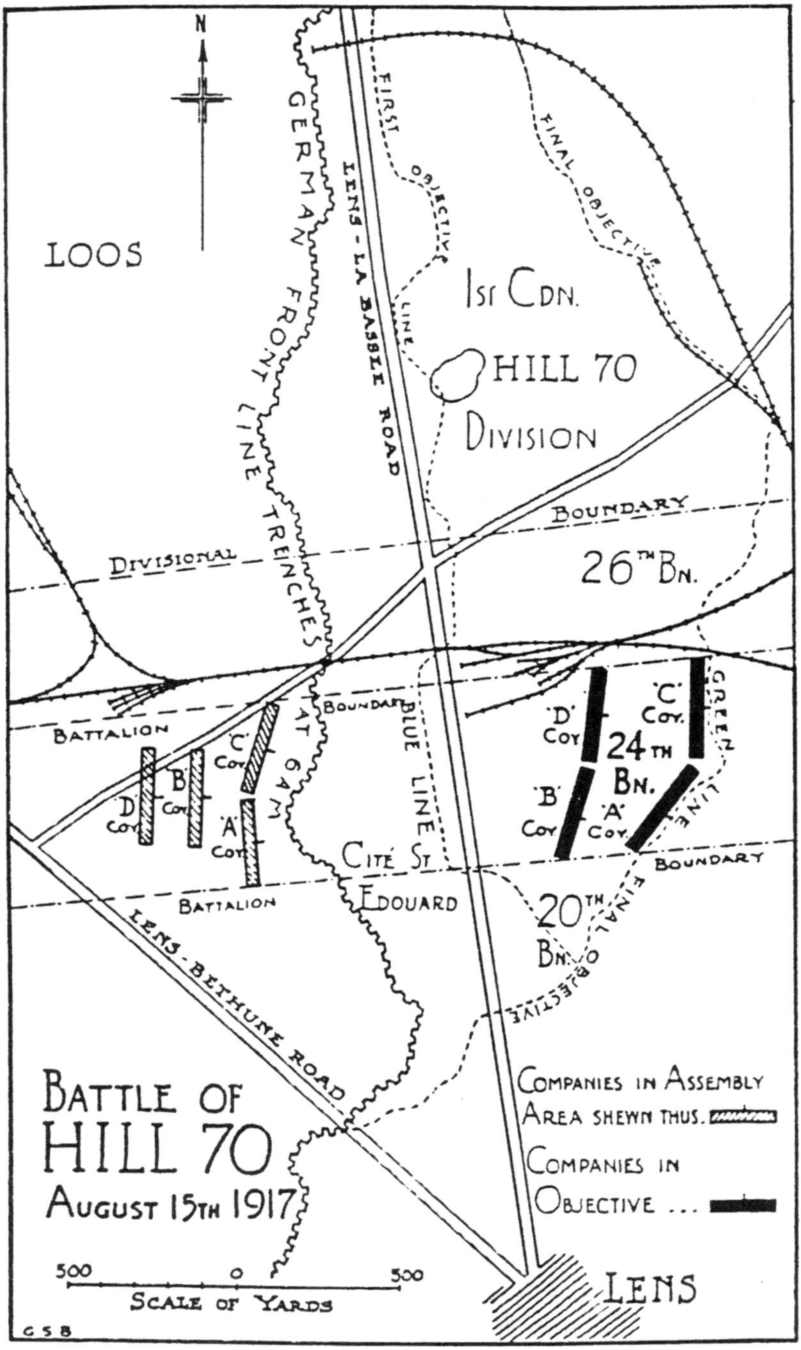
N
LOOS
GERMAN FRONT LINE TRENCHES
LENS - LA BASSEE ROAD
FIRST OBJECTIVE LINE
FINAL OBJECTIVE
1st CDN. HILL 70 DIVISION
DIVISIONAL BOUNDARY
26TH BN.
BATTALION BOUNDARY
AT 6 AM
BLUE LINE
GREEN LINE
'D' COY
'B' COY
'C' COY
'A' COY
24TH BN.
CITÉ ST EDOUARD
BATTALION BOUNDARY
20TH BN.
FINAL OBJECTIVE
LENS - BETHUNE ROAD
BATTLE OF HILL 70
AUGUST 15TH 1917
COMPANIES IN ASSEMBLY AREA SHEWN THUS.
COMPANIES IN OBJECTIVE ...
500 0 500
SCALE OF YARDS
LENS
GSB

newly-promoted General was allowed to shift the attack to his preferred target, Hill 70.

Hill 70 was a valuable height, but it was well-fortified, having been in German hands since 1914. It had been the rock against which the British attack at Loos in 1915 had been smashed and now, after two years of digging and tunnelling in the chalk subsoil, the Germans had made it an even more formidable position.

The Plan

Currie's plan was methodical and simple. His goal was to grab the hill and its surroundings (to provide a defensive perimeter) in a quick offensive thrust. He knew the Germans would pay a heavy price to retrieve it, counter-attacking with fearless abandon. Then it would be the turn of the Canadian artillery. The guns would be ranged on all possible routes and approaches that the Germans could use to launch counter-attacks. Currie's gunners would smash the Germans. His goals for Hill 70 were to kill Germans, provide a diversion for the forces in Flanders, and capture a strategic piece of territory. Hill 70 was Arthur Currie's battle. Success would depend on precise execution and infantry-artillery coordination. After a few postponements due to bad weather the date for the attack was finally set for August 15th, 1917.

Currie employed the techniques that had worked so well at Vimy. His men practised on a 'taped' battlefield at Aix-Noulette. He brought in 9 brigades of field artillery and had his gunners prepare a plan to target the German approaches and silence the enemy guns. Forty-eight heavy machine-gun crews would advance with the infantry to help stop enemy counter-attacks. Each platoon would be organized to operate independently as a defensive strong-point. They would bombard the enemy with smoke and burning oil drums to cover the infantry as they moved across No Man's Land. The 4th Division holding the rubble that was once the suburbs of Lens, would provide a diversionary attack.

His 1st Division, specifically Currie's old 2nd Brigade, would get the honour of taking Hill 70. They would be given the task of not only taking the Hill, but pushing 700 metres east and capturing the German second line. The 3rd Brigade would capture the woods north of Hill 70, Bois Rase, and Bois Hugo, and secure the approaches to the height. The 1st Brigade would be in reserve and be used as required, whenever and wherever the line was threatened.

The most difficult battlefield was given to the 2nd Division. They had to attack south of Hill 70 in the ruins of the old miners villages. These were now just heaps of old brick, but provided a maze of interconnecting basements for the Germans to use as defensive positions. Currie wanted the 2nd Division to advance almost 1.5 km through this rubble, to ensure the flanks of both attacking Divisions would conform. Any gap between them could give the Germans the opportunity to drive the Canadians back. This was the most vulnerable piece of his plan.

The 4th Division would provide a diversionary attack on August 15th, but they would also be required to attack as the battle took shape. The territory they faced was similar to that of the 2nd Division: ruins and rubble that were overlooked by the Germans who occupied the slag heaps that dominated the southern sector of Lens. Their battle would be fought hand-to-hand and house-to-house.

The Attack Goes In

At 4:25 am, following a rolling barrage, and covered by the smoke of burning oil barrels, the men of the 1st Division left their trenches. In less than 20 minutes they had crossed the Lens-La Bassee road and were in the German lines. The 7th and 10th Battalions had taken Hill 70. North of Hill 70 the 16th Battalion was in Bois Rase and the 15th was fighting through Bois Hugo. The first phase had gone perfectly. But now they had to wait 20 minutes for the rolling barrage to commence.

On the 2nd Division's front its attacking Battalions, north to south, 22nd, 25th, 20th, 21st, and 18th, had moved quickly to the attack and succeeded all along the line. They too were held up on their objectives waiting for the creeping barrage.

Finally they moved onto the second phase of the attack. East of Hill 70, the 5th, 8th and 7th Battalions moved down the slopes towards their final objective, the German trench running behind Hill 70. They met heavy machine-gun fire. In only 20 minutes the Germans had recovered from the initial blow and were now providing greater opposition. They suffered heavy casualties, but managed to gain most of their objectives, with a few exceptions. Now depleted, their attack on the Quarry was taken up by the 10th Battalion, who in desperate hand-to-hand fighting, captured this important position.

In the south the diversion by the 4th Division took place. They fired gas bombs and burning oil barrels into the German positions, and then

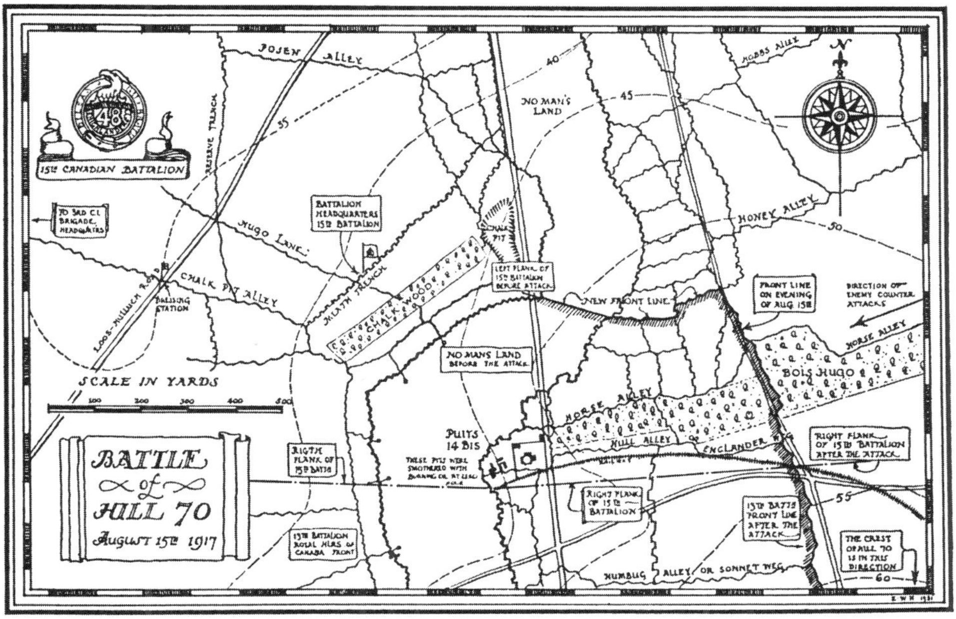

The most northern attack.

The ruins of Lens

sent out fighting patrols to test the German line. They found out the Germans were prepared to fight for every inch of Lens, and their patrols were driven back to the Canadian lines.

All along the line the Canadians now dug-in and prepared for the counter-attacks. By 9 am the Germans could be seen forming up to attack between Bois Hugo and the Quarry; but observers on Hill 70, and in the air, called in the artillery to break up the attack. The Germans were now being reinforced along the line, and their reserves were being rushed to the attack. At 11 am they tried again against Hill 70 with no success; and as the day wore into evening more German attacks were made. All failed.

On the afternoon of August 16th, 1917 the 5th and 8th Battalions tried to push on to capture the line they were unable to capture on the 15th, but their depleted ranks failed to grab the last pieces of the German second line.

The courage that marked the Canadian success at Vimy would also save the day at Hill 70. Six Victoria Crosses were awarded in the Battle of Hill 70, each act influenced the outcome of the battle. The 10th Battalion was cut off in the Quarry. All communications were down and they were facing a massive counter-attack. They had to send two runners up the machine-gun swept slope of Hill 70 to get the message through to the artillery. One runner was killed immediately, while the other, Private Harry Brown, though mortally wounded, made it to the crest and delivered his vital message. He collapsed on the steps of the dugout, and later died of his wounds. On the 7th Battalion front Private Michael O'Rourke, stretcher-bearer, twice went out and brought in wounded under heavy fire. Miraculously O'Rourke survived. *(Harry Brown, VC; born Gananoque, Ontario, May 10th,1898; died August 17th, 1917; buried Noeux-les-Mines Communal Cemetery, II.J.29. Michael James O'Rourke, VC; born Limerick, Ireland, March 19th, 1878; died Vancouver, British Columbia, December 6th, 1957.)*

On August 17th/18th the German counter-attacks intensified. They saturated the Canadian lines with Mustard Gas, and attacked. Three times they attacked the Chalk Quarry and were stopped. On the 2nd Division's sector they attacked the advanced positions of the 20th Battalion. During this action Sergeant Frederick Hobson took a Lewis Gun and fired point blank at the Germans. Later when the gun jammed, he attacked the Germans with his rifle, clubbing them, and driving them

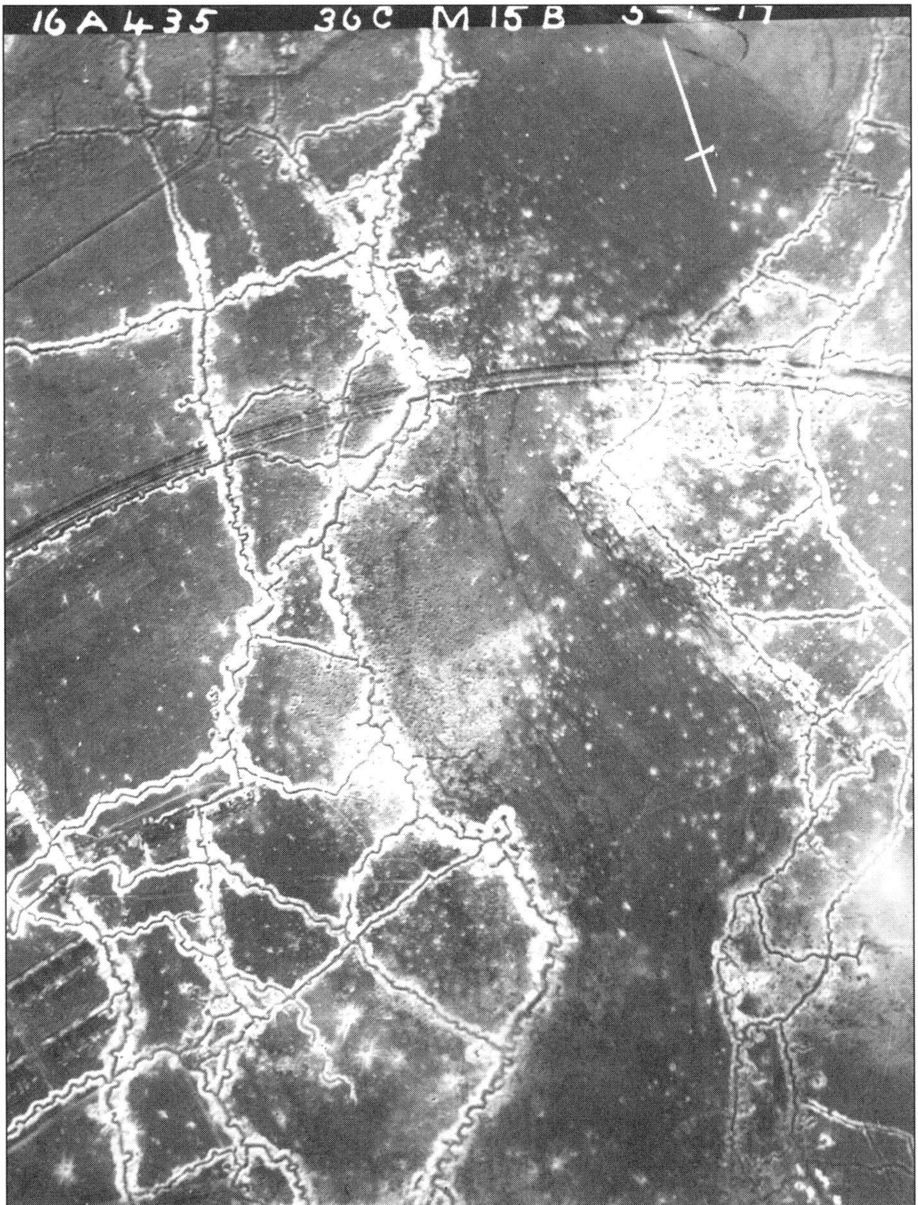

Aerial view of trench lines west of Lens, August 1917.

back. Hobson was shot and killed, but his courage saved the situation. Near Bois Hugo the Germans attacked the 2nd Battalion's positions and Major Okill Learmonth, MC, led the defence. Although wounded he stood on the parapet directing the attack, throwing back German grenades as they landed on their position. When his wounds became too serious he lay on the bottom of the trench and gave instructions for defence and the line held. Both Hobson and Learmonth won the Victoria Cross, posthumously. (*Frederick Hobson, VC; born Lincolnshire, November 23rd, 1875; died Lens, August 18th, 1917; no known grave, commemorated on the Vimy Memorial, France. Okill Massey Learmonth, VC, MC; born Quebec City, February 22nd, 1894; died August 19th, 1917; buried Noeux-les-Mines Communal Cemetery, II.K.9.)*

On August 21st, 1917 it was apparent that the Germans had conceded Hill 70 to the Canadians, and the counter-attacks ceased. In Lens the Canadians tried to improve their positions. There was a feeling that if they could capture the northern suburbs the Germans might evacuate the city. The planned night attack would cover the length of Lens from Cite St.Emile in the north to Cite Moulin in the south. The 27th (City of Winnipeg) and 29th (British Columbia) Battalions of the 2nd Division would attack in the north and the 4th Division, 50th (Alberta), 46th (Saskatchewan) and 47th (British Columbia) Battalions would attack in southern Lens. This night attack would be very difficult. The men had to fight in a destroyed city against an enemy who knew they were coming.

The 27th and 29th Battalions were able to advance quickly across 600 metres to Cinnabar Trench. But the 29th was caught between the Canadian and British barrages and came face to face with a German Guards battalion. The Germans were fought off in hand-to-hand combat, using bomb and bayonet. When all the officers were casualties, Company Sergeant Major Robert Hanna took over, and personally captured a German strong-point, killing four of the defenders. He then secured a section of Cinnabar Trench and held it against counter-attacks. Hanna was later awarded the Victoria Cross. By noon the Canadians were unable to secure the area. The 27th got to its objective but did not have sufficient men left to clear the Germans from the cellars and hidden trenches. In addition the failure of the 50th Battalion on their right, left them vulnerable. Finally the Canadians had to withdraw to their original positions. *(Robert Hill Hanna, VC; born Kilkeel, Ireland,*

Lens was almost entirely ringed round with solid concrete. The enemy even built concrete houses. This one has been blasted clean off its foundations by Canadian fire.

After the Canadians had captured Hill 70, the Germans made an abortive couter-attack. These wounded and captured Germans are waiting for "straf" to cease before proceeding to the Canadian rear.

August 6th, 1887; died Mount Lehman, British Columbia, June 15th, 1967.)

Although the 50th Battalion failed, the other two 4th Division Battalions moved the line forward 500 metres. When the 46th moved through the rubble they liberated a number of Canadians who had been trapped behind enemy lines on August 15th. The 47th advanced the furthest on the 21st, but to sustain its advances the men fought a bitter battle with the Germans, who held their positions often to the last man. In the ensuing struggles a Ukrainian Corporal, Filip Konowal, took out one machine-gun nest, and later single-handedly took on the Germans in two separate incidents. The next day he took out another machine-gun nest. Konowal was awarded the Victoria Cross for his bravery. *(Filip Konowal, VC; born Podolsky, Ukraine, September 15th, 1888; died Ottawa, Ontario, June 3rd, 1959.)*

On August 23rd, 1917 a single battalion operation against a German-held slag heap known as the Green Crassier (just south of the Lens train station) was undertaken by the 44th Battalion (Manitoba).If they could take and hold it, it would give the Canadians a strategic advantage over the enemy in southern Lens. To take the Green Crassier the 44th would have to advance 350 metres through the German lines, climb the Crassier, drive off the garrison, and hold it until relieved. In a brilliant action, the assault was launched at 3:00 am, and quickly the Manitobans secured their flank, climbed the Green Crassier, and took over. But the Canadians holding the approaches to the slag heap were forced to withdraw, leaving a company of the 44th isolated on the crest of the Crassier. Gradually the Germans closed in, supported by mortars and artillery. Fighting from improvised positions, the handful of men fought back doggedly, but time was not with them. By the late afternoon the Canadians were either dead or prisoners. The taking of the Green Crassier was a brilliant action, and with a little luck could have been a brilliant success. The 44th Battalion suffered 257 casualties, including 23 dead, 48 presumed dead, and 70 prisoners.

The final act in the battle of Hill 70/ Lens took place on August 25th, 1917, when the 50th Battalion, behind an effective barrage, captured Aloof Trench in western Lens with minimal casualties.

The Battle of Hill 70 was a great success and a trademark of the Canadians' planning and execution. The later attacks in the ruins of Lens were not as successful, but took place on an impossible battlefield.

None-the-less the Canadian Corps had much to be proud of. Their new Commander, Arthur Currie, had done well.

In the end Hill 70 worked as Currie planned it, but the cost was high. Canadian casualties were 9,198, including 2,400 dead. Within weeks the Canadian Corps would be on the move again, this time north, to Ypres, where the Canadians would encounter their greatest challenge of the war, the capture of Passchendaele.

"Faithful unto death"
Wounded runner dies as he delivers his message.

The Tour - Itinerary

Duration - 6 Hours

Point One: The 1st Canadian Division Enters the Line, March, 1915

Point Two: The Battle of Festubert, Attacks of May 16th-18th, 1915

Point Three: Canadian Orchard

Point Four: The Attacks of the 2nd Brigade Against K.5

Point Five; The Action of Givenchy, June 15th-16th, 1915

Point Six: The Battle of Loos, September, 1915

Point Seven: The Northern Assault, Bois Hugo, August 15th, 1917

Point Eight: The Northern Assault, Hill 70, August 15th, 1917

Point Nine: German Counter-Attacks, August 16th-18th, 1917

Point Ten: Driving Tour of Lens and the Green Crassier

The Tour

Fleurbaix - Festubert - Givenchy - Hill 70 - Lens

The Tour is designed to cover the first areas where the men of the 1st Canadian Division entered the line in February 1915, and the Battles of Festubert, Givenchy and Hill 70.

Leave Arras going north following the route to Bethune on the D937. The trip to Bethune is 26 km and you will pass through Souchez (10 km), Aix-Noulette (14 km), Sains-en Gohelle (18 km) and Noeux-les-Mines (22 km), before reaching the N41 just south of Bethune. Turn right on the N41 going east towards La Bassee, passing through Cambrin. After 7 km turn left on the D166 to Cuinchy, and cross the La Bassee Canal, and drive through Festubert. The road ends at the D171 (Rue du Bois). Turn right to Neuve Chapelle. After four km you reach the Indian Memorial (on your right).

The Memorial, located on a battle position known as Port Arthur, commemorates the Missing of the Indian Corps from their battles in 1914-15. The magnificent tigers were sculpted by Sir Charles Wheeler, brother of Victor Wheeler, who served with the Canadians and wrote *The 50th Battalion in No Man's Land* (CEF Books, 2000). There is Second World War battle damage on the monument, a reminder that the British fought in this area in their retreat to Dunkirk in May 1940. One hundred metres south of the Indian Memorial is the Portugese Cemetery. Portugal, Britain's oldest ally, had two Divisions in the field in 1917-18. They were wiped out in the German Offensive on the Lys River in April 1918. Both sites are worth a visit. As you drive on you will be crossing over the ground won by the British and Indians in the Battle of Neuve Chapelle, March 1915.

Continue across the D947 staying on the D171 through Neuve Chapelle (the area south of the road was where the western attack of the disastrous Battle of Aubers Ridge took place on May 9th, 1915) and you pass Fauquissart four km later. Four km later turn right towards Rue Petillon Military Cemetery (D174E). The road will become the D175 after two km. Stop at the cemetery and go to the southern wall overlooking the farmer's fields.

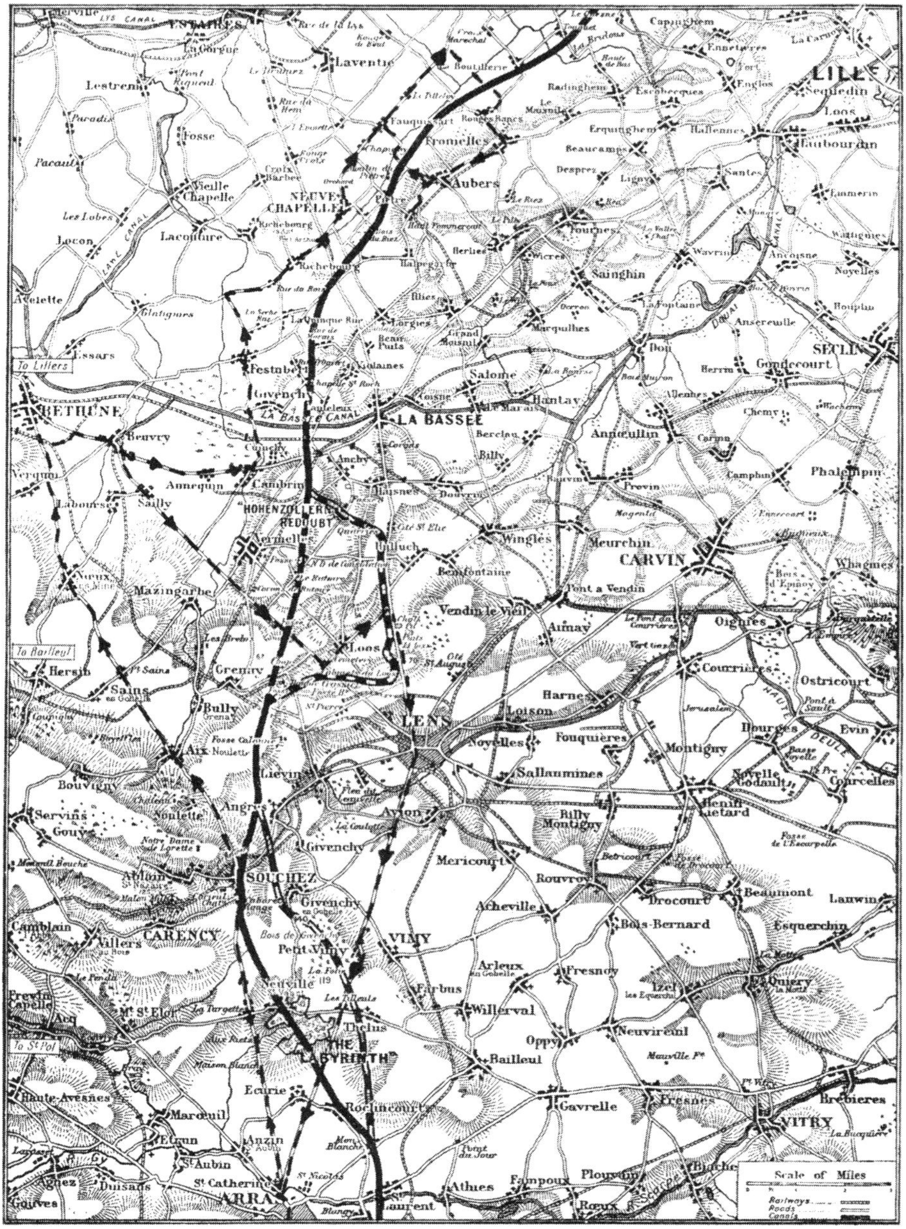
LYS CANAL
Estaires
La Gorgue
Laventie
Lestrem
Fauquissart
Fromelles
Aubers
Radinghem
Escobecques
Erquinghem
Hallennes
LILLE
Sequedin
Loos
Haubourdin
Beaucamps
Ligny
Santes
Emmerin
Fosse
Pacaut
Vieille Chapelle
NEUVE CHAPELLE
Richebourg
Lacouture
Locon
Les Lobes
Paradis
Fournes
Wavrin
Ancoisne
Wattignies
Noyelles
Sainghin
Marquillies
Illies
Herlies
Avelette
Essars
To Lillers
Festubert
Violaines
Givenchy
BETHUNE
Beuvry
LA BASSEE
Hantay
Salome
Don
Gondecourt
SECLIN
Annoeullin
Carvin
Phalempin
Verquin
Annequin
Cambrin
Auchy
Haisnes
Labourse
Sailly
HOHENZOLLERN REDOUBT
Vermelles
Hulluch
Wingles
Meurchin
CARVIN
Noeux
Mazingarbe
Benifontaine
Vendin le Vieil
Pont a Vendin
Oignies
To Bailleul
Hersin
Grenay
Loos
Courrières
Ostricourt
Sains en Gohelle
Bully Grenay
Harnes
LENS
Loison
Fouquières
Montigny
Evin
Aix Noulette
Lievin
Noyelles
Sallaumines
Courcelles
Bouvigny
Servins
Gouy
Noulette
Angres
Avion
Billy Montigny
Henin Lietard
Ablain St Nazaire
SOUCHEZ
Givenchy en Gohelle
Mericourt
Rouvroy
Drocourt
Beaumont
Lauwin
Camblain
Villers au Bois
CARENCY
VIMY
Acheville
Bois-Bernard
Esquerchin
Petit Vimy
Arleux en Gohelle
Fresnoy
Quiery la Motte
Neuville
Farbus
Willerval
Izel les Equerchin
Mt St Eloi
Thelus
THE LABYRINTH
Oppy
Neuvireuil
To St Pol
Bailleul
Haute-Avesnes
Ecurie
Roclincourt
Gavrelle
Fresnes
Brebieres
Marœuil
Etrun
Anzin
VITRY
St Aubin
Duisans
St Catherine
ARRAS
Athies
Fampoux
Plouvain
Roeux
Scale of Miles
Railways
Roads
Canals

The Tour – – →

Point One; The 1st Canadian Division Enters the Line, March, 1915.

When the 1st Canadian Division came into the line in March 1915 they held a four km sector extending from SE of Bois-Grenier (1st Brigade) to 500 metres south of Le Trou (3rd Brigade). The 2nd Brigade held the centre of the sector SE of Rue David. The trenches ran in a SE direction in the farmer's fields 400 metres from where you stand. The trenches were not in great shape. The majority were built-up sandbag walls and many could not stop a bullet. The Canadian inexperience, and the poor defences, resulted in many Canadian casualties due to sniping.

On March 10th, 1915 the Canadians made a "show" to deflect German attention from the attack on Neuve Chapelle. In the month spent on the Bois-Grenier-Fleurbaix-Laventie line they suffered 371 casualties. The 1st Canadian Division was moved north to Ypres in mid-April, 1915.

Return to your car and continue on the D175 to Le Trou Aid Post Cemetery. It is one of the most beautiful cemeteries in France. It is on an island (with ducks in the moat), surrounded by weeping willows and contains several early Canadian graves. It was 500 metres behind the Canadian front line. After a visit to Le Trou and a few obligatory photographs, turn left on the D22c to Fromelles.

You are crossing two battlefields, Aubers Ridge, May 9th, 1915, and Fromelles, where on July 19th/20th, 1916 Australian and British troops launched an attack on the German lines. Fromelles was supposed to be a diversionary attack to draw German reserves from the Somme front. It was a failure. The German domination of Aubers Ridge and their deep defensive positions crushed the attack. The losses were 5,533 Australian and 1,547 British casualties for no gain. It was the Australians' first battle since the Gallipoli evacuation.(See *Guide to Australian Battlefields of the Western Front, 1916-1918* by John Laffin, Kangaroo Press, 1992.) You will be reminded of this when you pass the Australian cemetery, V.C. Corner, and the Australian Battlefield Park and Memorial. The former was in No Man's Land and the latter was the German front line.

V.C. Corner is a unique cemetery containing 410 unmarked, individual graves of Unknown Australian Soldiers. The screen walls at the north end of the cemetery list the names of 1,299 Australian soldiers killed at Fromelles and who have no known grave. In this area there area dozens of bunkers to be seen in the fields (three are in the Australian

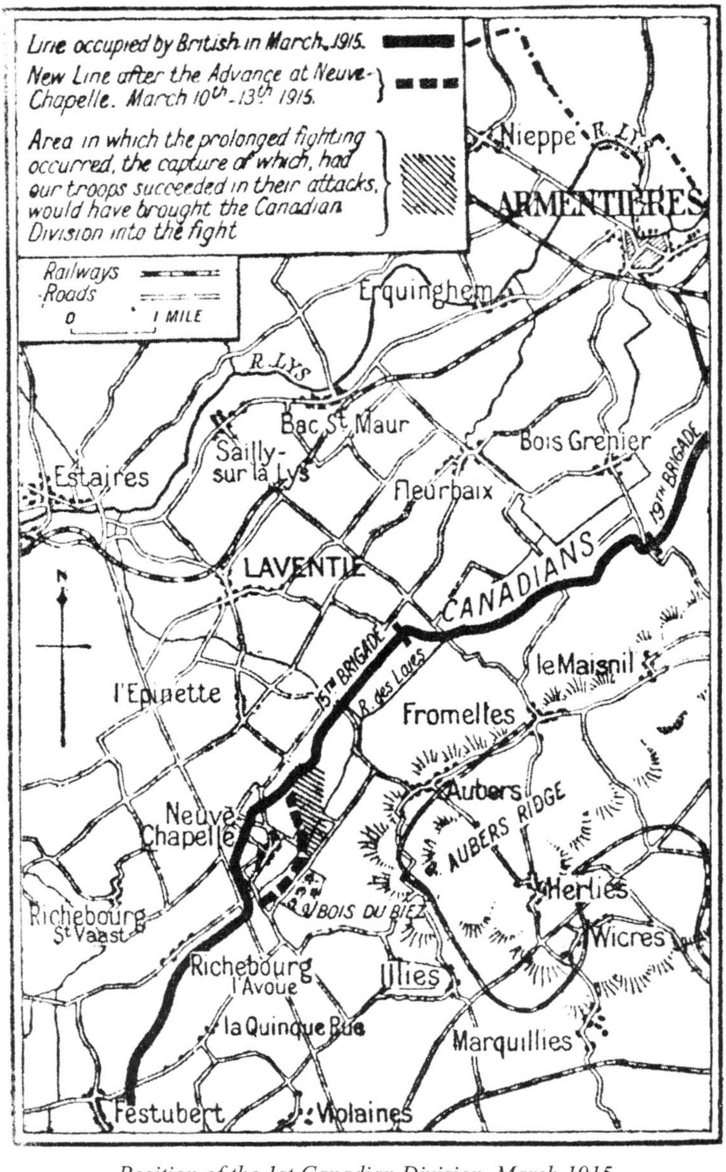

Position of the 1st Canadian Division, March 1915.

Rue Petillon Military Cemetery. (Christie)

View East from Rue Petillon Military Cemetery. (Christie)

Park) and the remnants of battle can be found by the least observant shrapnel-baller.

Drive into Fromelles, ascending the Aubers Ridge, into the village. At the 'T' junction turn right on the D141 to Aubers. You are driving along the Aubers Ridge and it is easy to see why it was so important. It is the most dominant height in the area, and commands a tremendous view of the British lines. From this advantageous position the Germans could observe any movement and instantly call artillery fire on any target. It is easy to see why the Battles of Aubers Ridge and Fromelles were such easy victories for the Germans.

Five hundred metres out of Fromelles a German bunker appears on the right. This was used by Adolf Hitler during the First World War. Hitler visited the bunker in June 1940 after accepting the surrender of France at Compiegne. It was at this time he also visited the Vimy Memorial.

Drive past Aubers (note all the pillboxes in the fields, including the one shaped like a house at the junction with the D41), and turn right on the D41 on the western end of the village. The road descends the Ridge and jogs to the right where it becomes the D173. When you reach the D171 at Fauquissart, turn left to Neuve Chapelle (you will retrace your steps to Festubert), crossing the D947, and then turning left on the D166. At Festubert turn left on the D72 (La Quinque Rue) and after 1.5 km stop your car.

Point Two; The Battle of Festubert, Attacks of May 16th-18th, 1915

This point gives a clear view of the battlefield, north and south. There are no landmarks, and it is understandable why the attackers had such a hard time directing their assaults. Festubert is an ugly battlefield. It also gives views to the south where you can see the Double Crassier at Loos, and to the north, on a clear day, you can see Mont Kemmel (south of Ypres).

You are standing on the line captured by the British on May 16th. On the 17th they continued their attack against the trench redoubt, the Quadrilateral, one km NE, and the fortified Ferme du Bois (1.5 km NE). The North Breastwork ran from the old German frontline to the Orchard (1,200 metres), 200 metres south of La Quinque Rue. When the Canadians were ordered into the line they were to capture the North

Festubert Church. (Christie)

View of Canadian Orchard (in centre) from Festubert Village. (Christie)

Breastwork, and advance to the German line that ran north from the Orchard to Ferme du Bois.

The attack by the 14th Battalion took place in the fields north of you. Without much protection the Montrealers were shot down in the fields, but advanced the line 200 yards. The attack by the 16th Battalion on the North Breastwork was more successful. They tried a two-pronged approach: attacking from the north across the fields where you are standing, and another assault coming from the south. They managed to hold part of the line. The fighting continued on until the 19th, when the Canadians attacked again.

Return to your car and drive on for 800 m and turn right on a small road D167E towards a campsite. Stop in front of the campsite.

Point Three: Canadian Orchard

This campsite was the location of Canadian Orchard, so called after its capture by the 16th Battalion. On May 20th the 16th continued their assault towards the Orchard, and took it. In the Battle of Festubert the 16th suffered 277 casualties. At the same time as the assault on the Orchard the 15th Battalion captured the rest of the North Breastwork. The Germans counter-attacked but could not dislodge the Highlanders. On May 24th the 3rd Battalion attacked east of the Orchard (what would be the back of the campsite) and some of the men broke into the German line. But they could not be reinforced and all of them were killed or captured. At the end of the battle Canadian Orchard became the new frontline and it remained the frontline until 1918.

Return to your car and drive on 400 m, taking the sharp right on the D167E (Rue D'Ouvert) to Givenchy. The road takes a sharp jog to the left, and just past the hamlet, Rue D'Ouvert, stop.

Point Four: The Attacks of the 2nd Brigade Against K.5

You are standing at the point where the South Breastwork crossed the road. The position itself extended 900 metres into the fields to the west. You also get a clear view of Festubert village. The frontlines ran in the middle of the fields between you and Festubert village. Arthur Currie's 2nd Brigade was given the task of capturing the South Breastwork, and specifically, a Strong-point, K.5, built into the Breastwork. After a few days of shelling the battlefield was a mess and Currie could not determine exactly where K.5 was. From your vantage-point it is easy to understand the confusion and also the task of the men who had to attack

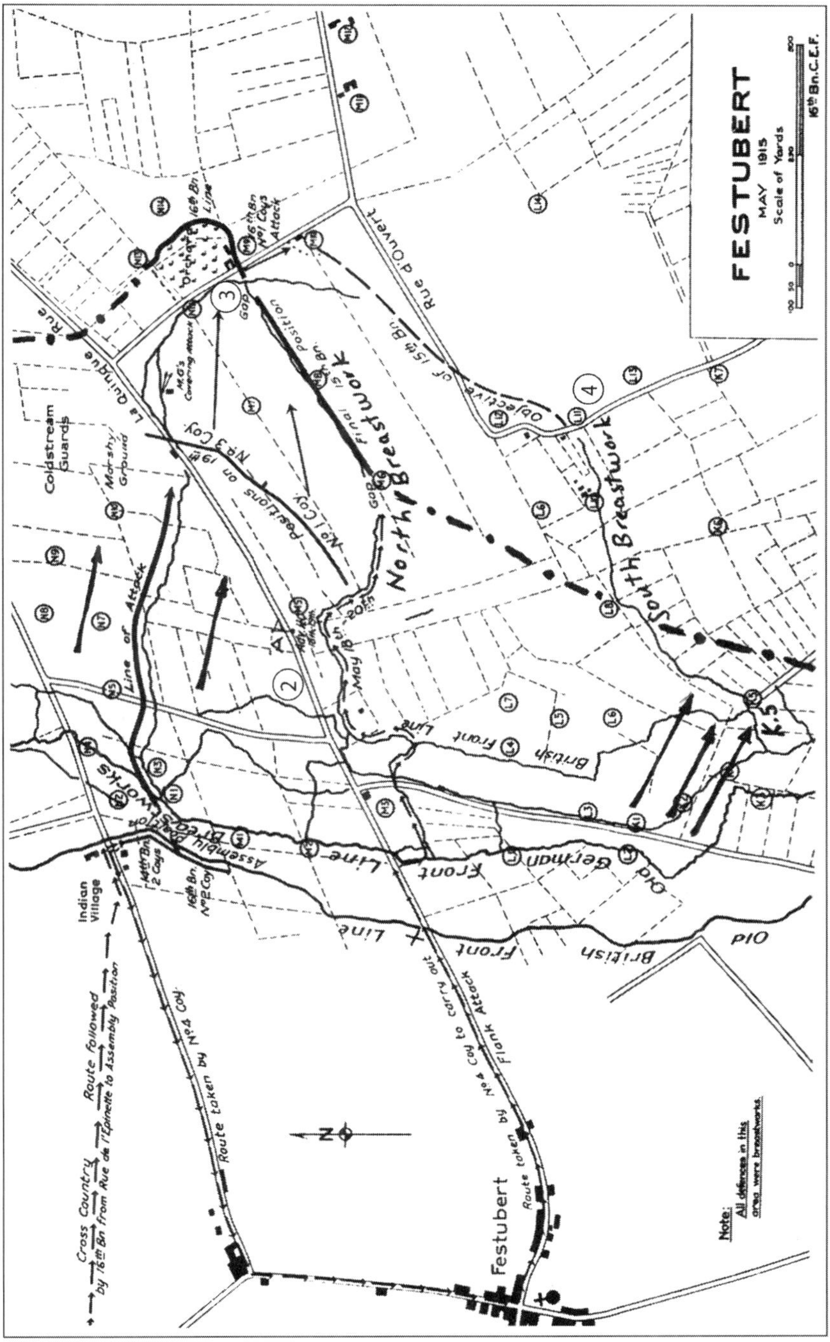

Tour Points (2), (3), *and* (4).

Innes-Hopkins, Captain James Randolph, 5th Battalion, C.E.F., youngest son of William Randolph Innes Hopkins of Malton, by his wife Evereld Eliza; born at Grey Towers, Cleveland, 5 Oct. 1876; educated at Oriel College, Oxford; served in the South African War, 1899-1902, as a trooper and was afterwards given a commission in the Northumberland Hussars; went to Canada in 1906, and settled in Saskatchewan. On the outbreak of war he immediately offered his services and was given a commission as Captain 22 Sept, 1914. Came over with the First Contingent and was stationed on Salisbury Plain during the winter of 1914-15; went to France in Feb. and was killed in action at Festubert, 24 May 1915, while leading his men. He is buried in Le Touret Military Cemetery, II.B.15. Captain Hopkins' two nephews, Lieutenant Charles Innes Hopkins and Private Castell Innes Hopkins were both killed in action. Charles was killed 18 Dec. 1914 with the Cameronians, and is buried in Royal Irish Rifles Graveyard, Laventie, and Castell was killed at Loos, 25 Sept. 1915, serving with the Gordon Highlanders, and is commemorated on the Loos Memorial. Captain Innes Hopkins married in London, 29 Sept. 1904, Doreen Maud Parker and they had a daughter, Evereld, 1905.

Andrew, Private Frederick Russell; 16th Battn, Canadian Scottish, C.E.F.; son of Capt. James and Sarah Andrew of Owen Sound, Ontario; born Owen Sound, 1 July 1885; educated Owen Sound Collegiate; enlisted at Victoria Sept. 1914; and went to France in Feb. 1915; died of shrapnel wounds 9 June 1915, received at the Battle of Festubert; unmarried. Lieut. H.A. Colquhoun wrote; "'Happy,' as he was called by the men, came through the fight in the Orchard, where he did exceedingly well, being very courageous and cool under the most trying fire. After this attack we were in reserve behind our former position. We were all out in the open when the Germans put six shrapnel shells among us. I managed to get to a dugout with Capt. Morison, when Andrew came in wounded. I remember well he had some flesh wounds in his back, but one bad one in the left breast. At the time he was being bandaged up I tried to hold his head on my knee, but he seemed to want to get up and walk. He was a splendidly strong man, and we all thought he was quite safe; but I fear that shot in the left breast was worse than we thought. On making inquiries I find that he passed away without pain about 9 June.

across these open fields. The 10th Battalion tried to take K.5 on May 20th, but were shot down. They tried again on the 21st with a little more success. They got into the position, but were later forced to retire after heavy shelling.

On May 24th Currie tried again, using the 5th and 7th Battalions, and this time they captured K.5. The losses of the 10th and 5th Battalions in capturing K.5 were 268 and 250 respectively. The next day men of the Lord Strathcona's Horse tried to advance down the South Breastwork, to another redoubt, known as M.10. They failed to take it. The South Breastwork was not captured in its entirety until the general advance to victory in September 1918.

As you will notice there is little evidence of the fighting that took place here, with the exception of a few barbed-wire stakes.

Continue on until you reach the junction with the D167. After 1.2 km turn left on the D167 and continue to Givenchy (900 metres). At Givenchy you will see the Memorial to the 55th West Lancashire Division and a small wooded area to your left. Stop and walk into the wooded area.

Point Five; The Action of Givenchy, June 15th-16th, 1915

This Memorial Park commemorates the heroic action of the 55th West Lancashire Division in the Great War. It was built over the British second line position; and if you walk to the north side of the Park you will get a clear view of the Canadian battlefield of June 15th-16th, 1915.

What is immediately obvious is how flat the land is and what an advantage the Germans had. Although the fields are full of battlefield relics there is nothing about the place that helps with understanding the battle. You have to imagine two trench lines running north-south, only 75 metres apart at some points. The Canadian 18 pounders that were brought into the line would have been placed where the British trenches would cut the D167. They opened fire at the German strong-points, and got off 120 rounds before they were put out of action. At 5:58 pm a mine was blown, short of the German line, killing a number of Canadians. The 1st Battalion stormed across No Man's Land, reaching the German line, and pushing into the second line 200 metres further on. Their attack took place in a NE direction, from a jump-off point roughly where you are standing.

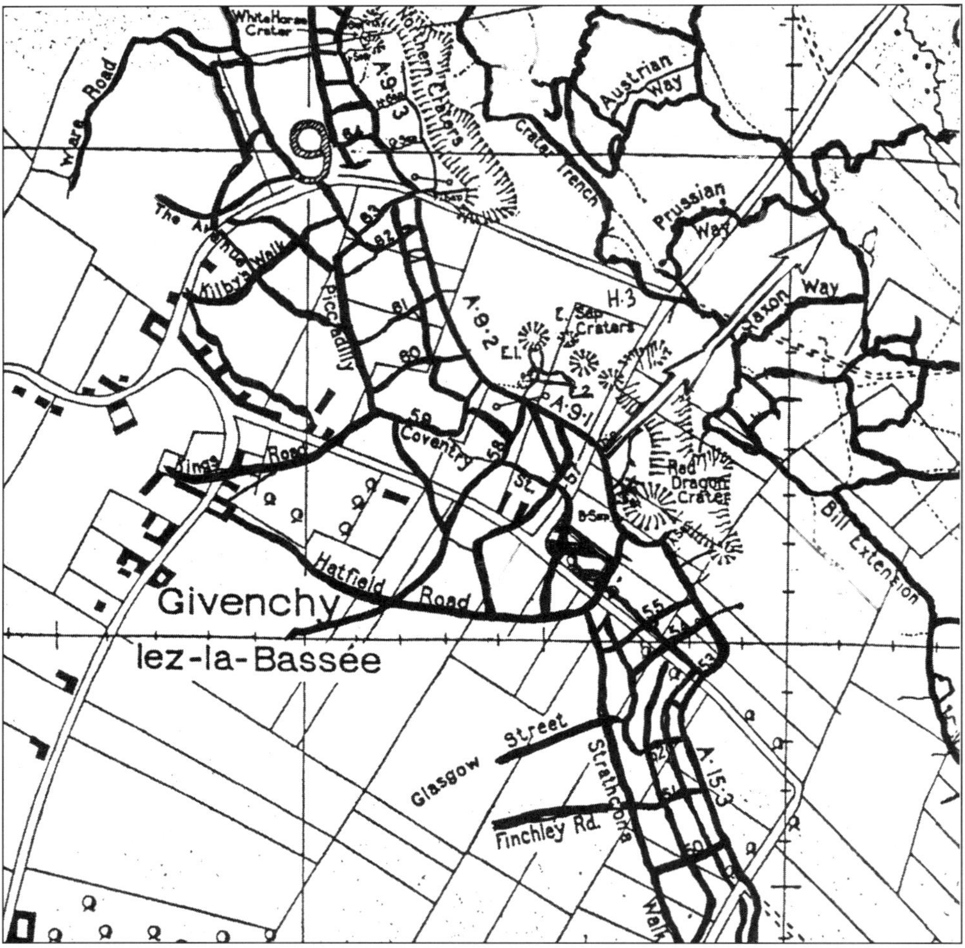

The Givenchy Battlefield. The arrow marks the Canadian attacks. The cross-hatched area is the 55th Division Memorial Park.

Lieutenant Craig directing the fire of an 18-pounder gun against the enemy's trenches, June 15th, 1915.

The Givenchy Battlefield today. The Canadians' attack crossed the field near the tractor on the left. (Christie)

It was near here that Frederick Campbell decided to take his machine-gun forward across No Man's Land and into the German line, to help his trapped comrades. His VC would have been won about 300 metres NE of your position. Somehow the men brought back the mortally wounded officer, as they fell back to their front line. By 11 pm it was all over. The small venture had cost the 1st Battalion (Western Ontario) 386 casualties.

The next day the 3rd Battalion tried the same operation, but could not even get into the enemy positions. The Second Action of Givenchy was over. It cost the Canadians 300 dead.

After the fighting in 1915 this area quieted down and over the next three years the front lines never changed. As with anywhere on the Western Front, there were always deaths due to snipers or shelling. At Givenchy there was a considerable amount of mining. In June 1916 the Germans blew a mine under a Welsh position just north of this Park. It was known as "Red Dragon Crater". In 1925 the remains of two Welsh officers killed in the blast were discovered. They were re-interred in Cabaret Rouge British Cemetery (see *The War The Infantry Knew* by Captain J.C. Dunn).

In April 1918 the German Offensive on the Lys was halted at Givenchy by the magnificent defence put up by the 55th West Lancashire Division. The Germans broke through from south of Ypres to Givenchy, penetrating to the outskirts of Bethune. But the 55th held. They smashed a frontal assault by five German Divisions. Consequently this location for their Memorial could not be more appropriate.

You may also want to visit the Communal Cemetery which contains the graves of 30 British soldiers killed in the retreat to Dunkirk in 1940. There is also the grave of a Soviet soldier killed in September 1944 when this area was liberated by the Allies. He was probably with a Communist Circuit of the French resistance.

Return to your car and drive into Givenchy, marked by the unusual church and continue to the D166. Turn left on the D166 crossing over the La Bassee Canal. When you reach the N41 and turn right for Bethune, and pass through Cambrin. When you reach the eastern outskirts of Bethune turn left on the N43 to Lens. Pass through Noyelles, Mazingarbe, and after 8 km Dud Corner Cemetery appears on the rise on your left. Pull over at the cemetery, and climb the stairs to the observation platform to the left of the entrance to the cemetery.

Point Six: The Battle of Loos, September, 1915

The view from the observation platform is terrific. You get a great view of the Loos battlefield of 1915. To the SW you can see Notre Dame De Lorette and the top of the Canadian Monument at Vimy Ridge. Looking NE across the fields the village of Hulluch is four km away. The infamous Hohenzollern Redoubt and Fosse 8 are also four km NE of Dud Corner. The cemetery was built on what was the German frontline on September 25th, 1915. Looking east Loos village is in the hollow, 1.5 km away. The high point of Hill 70 is 3.2 km east. It is where the La Bassee-Lens road reaches its highest point, and is marked by traffic lights.

In the 1915 battle British troops attacked from west of the Bethune-Lens road, surged into Loos village, and advanced onto Hill 70. To the NW they also captured the Hohenzollern Redoubt. They could not hold these positions. Over the next few days the Germans retook Hill 70, and the positions along the La Basse-Lens road. The British Army lost 50,000 men in the battle.

In 1917 the line the Canadians held was in the fields east of Loos village, and west of the La Bassee-Lens road.

Continue on the N43 towards Lens, turning left into the village of Loos (after 1.4 km). Continue through the village on the D165. When it meets the D947 turn right and after 1.3 km turn left, just past the airfield. There is parking in the Park to the left of the road. Stop at the parking lot.

Point Seven: The Northern Assault, Bois Hugo, August 15th, 1917.

This is the northern flank of the Canadian attack on August 15th, 1917. The 15th Battalion (48th Highlanders of Toronto) attacked from the other side of the old mining pithead, Puits No. 14, to the west of you. They stormed across the road and advanced 500 metres into Bois Hugo. Today the Canadian half of Bois Hugo is the parking lot. They stopped and dug in literally at the eastern end of the parking lot. The Germans held the wooded area, Parc des Cytises. From there the Germans launched several counter-attacks. The 2nd Battalion (Eastern Ontario) relieved the 15th in the Wood, and in the fields south of it. It was in the field just south of Bois Hugo where Okill Learmonth, MC, won his Victoria Cross.

In the fields south of you the 13th Battalion swept across the

The Battle of Loos, September 25th - October 8th, 1915

After the battles of the spring of 1915 the British Army had been weakened, and newly-arrived troops and guns were insufficient to launch a large attack. However, the French, who were planning a major offensive in Artois and Champagne, pressured the British to assist them with an attack of their own. Politically they forced the British to agree for a September attack near Loos. For the assault the British would use chlorine gas, and six British Divisions would launch an attack from west of the Lens-Bethune road. The attack went in on September 25th, 1915. The first stages of the attack went well, with some exceptions where the gas blew back on British troops, but by the early morning they had carried the first line, and had captured Loos village and the Hohenzollern Redoubt. Some were pushing on to Hill 70.

With things going well two other Divisions were sent in to exploit the success, but the new men were advancing in unknown terrain, without any landmarks. By this time the Germans were quickly bringing up reserves and counter-attacking. By September 26th the Germans had retaken Hill 70. British attacks continued across the open ground between Hill 70 and Hulluch, but the men were decimated by shell and machine gun fire. Confusion about the situation, due to a lack of communication and inexperience, severely affected the command decisions, and as the British Generals hesitated the Germans struck back, regaining some of the lost territory.

On September 27th the British renewed their offensive, attacking across the open fields north of Hill 70, with predictable results. Despite the courage of the men they could make no inroads, and were fortunate to hold some of the gains of September 25th. By nightfall of the 27th the attackers were exhausted, and could no longer continue the offensive.

On October 8th the Germans counter-attacked without gaining much ground, and on October 13th the British launched another attack, but it failed. The Battle of Loos cost the British Army 50,000 casualties, of which 16,000 were killed, for an advance of three km. The frontline would remain static until the Canadians attacked in August 1917.

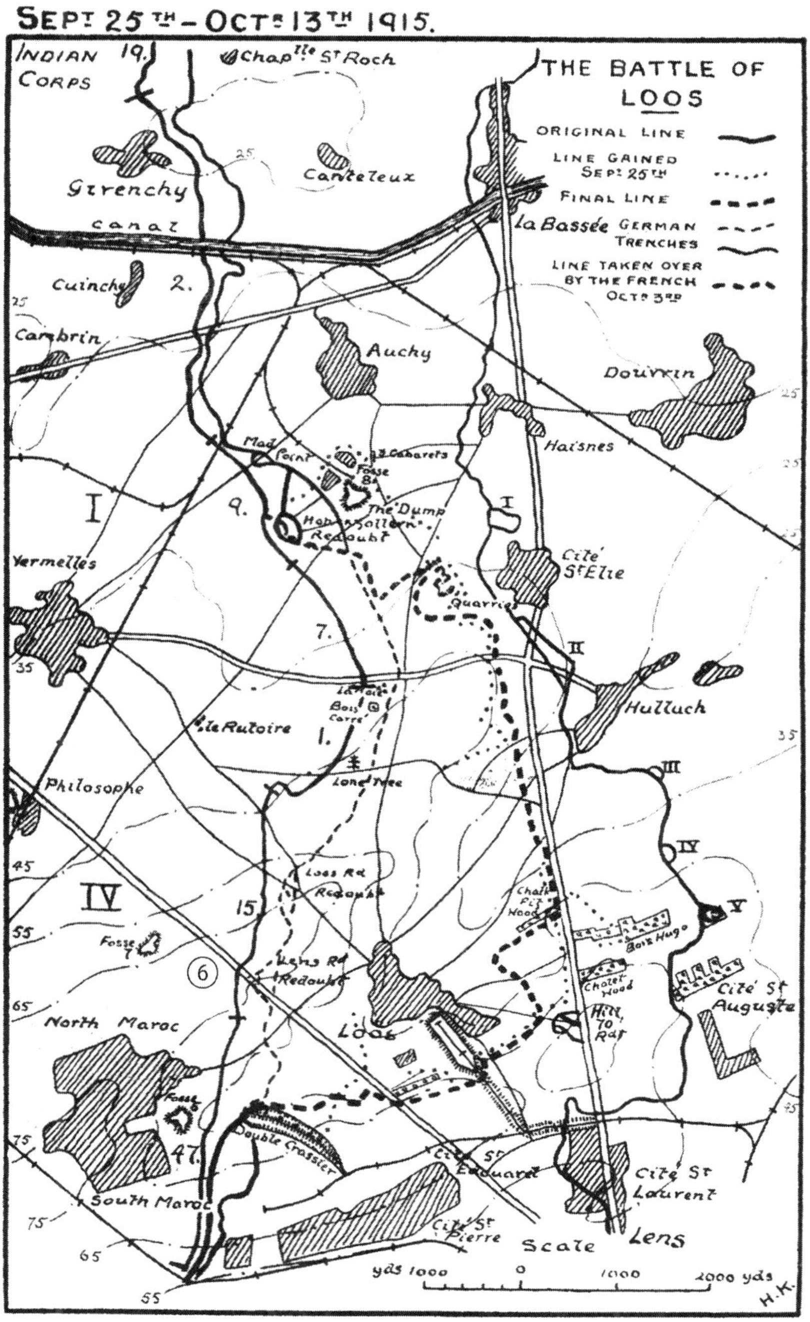
SEPT 25TH - OCTR 13TH 1915.
THE BATTLE OF LOOS
ORIGINAL LINE
LINE GAINED SEPT 25TH
FINAL LINE
GERMAN TRENCHES
LINE TAKEN OVER BY THE FRENCH OCT 3RD
INDIAN CORPS
19.
Chapelle St Roch
Givenchy
Canteleux
canal
La Bassée
Cuinchy
2.
Cambrin
Auchy
Douvrin
Haisnes
Mad Point
Fosse 8
The Dump
Hohenzollern Redoubt
I
9.
Vermelles
Cité St Elie
Quarries
7.
II
Hulluch
Le Rutoire
1.
Lone Tree
Philosophe
III
IV
Loos Rd Redoubt
Chalk Pit Wood
V
15.
Bois Hugo
Fosse 7
6
Lens Rd Redoubt
Chalet Wood
Cité St Auguste
Hill 70
North Maroc
Loos
Fosse 5
47.
Double Crassier
Cité St Edouard
Cité St Laurent
South Maroc
Cité St Pierre
Scale
Lens
yds 1000
0
1000
2000 yds
H.K.

Tour Point (6).

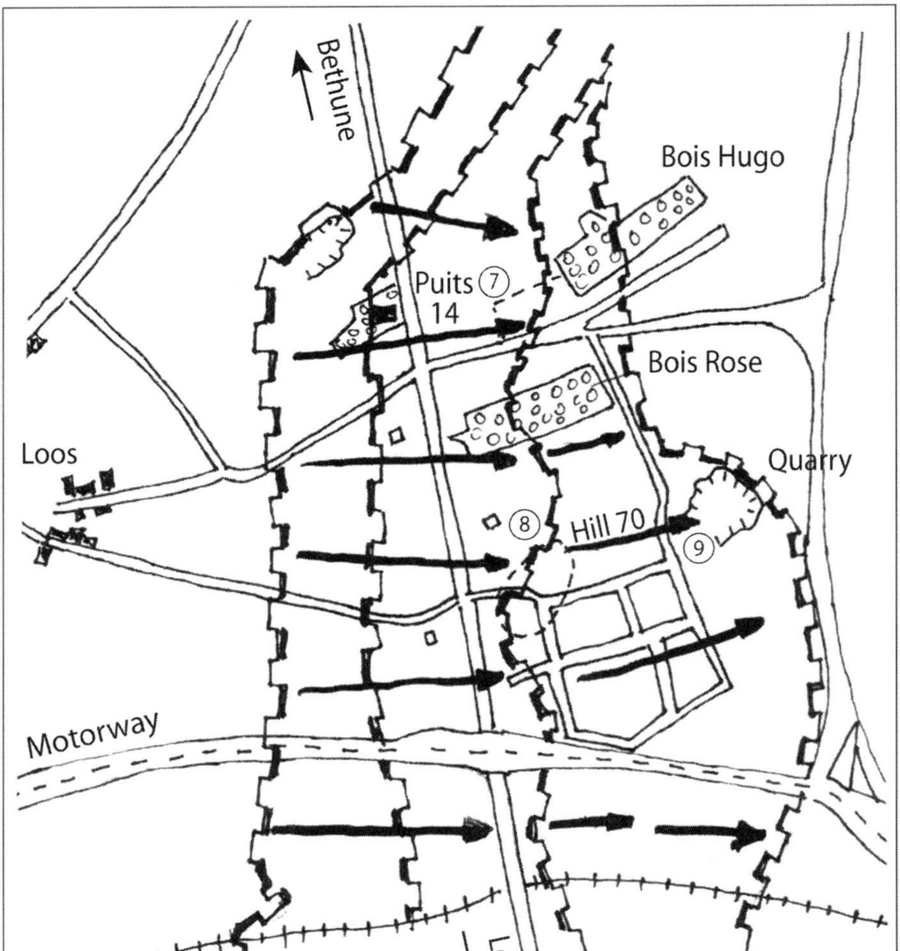

The Northern Attack, August 15th, 1917.
Tour Points ⑦, ⑧, *and* ⑨.

Bethune-Lens road and secured the line between Bois Hugo and Bois Rase.

The N43 is a very busy road, so it is suggested to walk this part of the tour. Walk over to the N43, and go south (left) towards the high point on the N43, one km distant, marked by the traffic lights. That high point is Hill 70. Walk towards Hill 70.

You will see a few German pillboxes on both sides of the road, that mark their first and second lines. The Canadian jump-off line ran north-south in the fields 500 metres to the west, in front of Loos village. As you walk up the road the wood on your left is Bois Rase. It was captured by the 16th Canadian Scottish on August 15th. They captured the entire Wood, and linked up with the Canadian advances on their flanks. You will pass the Crematorium, and ahead of you, to the left is a German pill-box. It's off in the field, so you may want to stay on the roadside.

Point Eight: The Northern Assault, Hill 70, August 15th, 1917.

From this position you can look south to see the crest of Hill 70. The building on the crest is a Children's Daycare facility, and the wooded area that surmounts the crest was the objective of the 10th Battalion (Alberta) and the 7th Battalion (British Columbia). The 10th captured the pillbox you are standing by, and the 7th passed through to take the crest and advance 500 metres down the eastern slope. Both attacks were very successful.

Further south of Hill 70 the 8th Battalion (Winnipeg) kept up with the advances of the other battalions. The first assaults of the 1st Division had gone according to plan. They how to secure the eastern perimeter around Hill 70 and prepare for counter-attacks.

Return to your car. Drive south towards Lens and when you reach Hill 70 (at the traffic lights) turn left on the small road that loops around the Children's Daycare, the crematorium, the airport and the industrial park.

Point Nine: German Counter-Attacks, August 16th-18th, 1917.

You are driving along the crest of Hill 70. The 7th Battalion advanced over this territory on August 15th.

When you hit a 'T' junction turn left, and drive 150 metres and stop.

Looking west you can see the crest of Hill 70. The Quarry was immediately off the road to your right, and was filled in 1995. The barren

Hill 70 today. The Woods and the traffic lights mark the crest. (Christie)

View north of Hill 70 towards Puits 14. (Christie)

slope leading to Hill 70 was where two Canadian Victoria Crosses were won. Michael O'Rourke, the stretcher-bearer, won his for treating the wounded in the open on these slopes. It was also across these fields that Harry Brown, the runner, did his courageous act. There was hand-to-hand fighting in the Quarry, and all communication was cut. The 10th was running low of ammunition and desperately needed artillery support. Brown had to carry the message up the shell and machine-gun swept slope to get through. The other runner with him was killed, and Brown, although mortally wounded, delivered his message.

Drive on looking east.

The final Canadian advances on August 16th took place in the fields on your right. The dozens of German counter-attacks were made against these positions. The Germans launched their attacks from what is now an Industrial Park. Ironically there is a McDonald's on the old German second line.

You will pass the Bois Rase on your left, and the road ends at Bois Hugo (on the spot where the 2nd Battalion fought off the counter-attacks and Learmonth won his VC).

Point Ten: Driving Tour of Lens and the Green Crassier

At this point the tour of the battlefield becomes more difficult. The fighting in Lens was done in a built-up area, of railways, industrial buildings, and the rubble of the miner's homes. Today it has all been rebuilt and is a crowded city. It is possible to revisit the areas where the battles were fought, but very difficult to get a sense of them. For example two Canadian VCs, Bob Hanna and Frederick Hobson, were won near the community swimming pool. The next section is the driving tour.

Return to the N43 turning left for Lens. You will pass over the motorway (A21), where the 5th and 8th Battalions attacked. Keep driving straight into Lens. Once you pass over the Railway you cross into the battlefield of the 2nd Canadian Division.

The 22nd Battalion attacked along the railway and across this road. The 26th Battalion took over attacking east of the road, towards a main German trench known as Nun's Alley, 800 metres to the east. It was the objective of the 2nd Division and the scene of fierce fighting. Fighting in ruins gave a great advantage to the enemy who could hide in basements and attack from the rear. Mopping up parties would have the task of eliminating these pockets of resistance. The house-to-house battles must have been Canada's First World War's Ortona.

View towards Canadian lines from Hill 70. German bunker in mid-distance. (Christie)

View west towards Loos village from Hill 70. (Christie)

Driving on a further 700 metres you are crossing the path of the 20th Battalion (Toronto) as it attacked on August, 15th. You can turn left on Rue Robert Schurman and follow it into the city. It was the location of heavy fighting, but there is absolutely no evidence of war. Follow Rue Schurman 800 metres until you reach the Community Swimming Pool.

It was just north of here that Frederick Hobson won his Victoria Cross beating off German counter-attacks. Hobson was killed in the action and his body was not found after the war.

To the south of the Pool was the area where the 29th Battalion fought on August 21st, 1917 and where they fought a hand-to-hand battle with a German Guards Battalion. It was also in this area Bob Hanna won his Victoria Cross. Cinnabar Trench and Nun's Alley were the objectives for the attack on the 21st. The Canadians reached both positions but were unable to hold them.

Turn around and return to the N43, turning left (south). Go under the railway (you are now in the 4th Canadian Division's area of attack) keeping left, and turn left (south) at the first main road, Route D'Arras. After 700 metres you can see the Green Crassier on your left, behind a few small factories.

On your right is where the 47th Battalion (British Columbia) attacked on August 21st, 1917, and it was in this area that Flilip Konowal won his VC.

To visit the Green Crassier, turn left at a small industrial estate, onto Rue du Grossouvre and follow the road up a hill. The 44th Battalion attacked the Green Crassier across this road, and then climbed up its steep sides and captured the summit. Where the road ends turn left, and then take a sharp right on Rue Thomas Edison. Follow Rue Thomas Edison as it curves around the Green Crassier. It leads over the Motorway, but turn right BEFORE the road crosses over the Motorway. This road leads to parking lot and it is an easy walk to the summit of the Green Crassier. Today the slag heaps known as Crassiers are called in French a kinder, gentler word, Terrils. The area is a bit creepy, but the local Police have advised it is safe.

Once on top you get an understanding of how tremendous the 44th's action was. You can see Lens Railway Station to the north, as well as the old mining pithead, known as Fosse St. Louis in the Great War. You can

Ruins of Lens.

Ruins of Lens.

also see the surrounding city, and understand how difficult it would have been to attack in this area. A brief look around also gives a clear understanding as to why Arthur Currie did not want to launch his main attack here. You can get a more commanding view of the surrounding area, including Vimy, by climbing the Crassier in the Park (Parc de la Glissoire) across the Motorway. To get there return to the Rue Thomas Edison and turn right, going over the Motorway. There is parking on the other side and you can walk to the top of Fosse No. 5.

Return to the N43 and turn left at the small Industrial Estate, in one km you will reach the N17. Follow it back to Arras. You will drive through the Avion-Mericourt sector (the scene of heavy fighting for the Canadians in May-July 1917) and across the Douai plain where the Canadians fought in the spring and summer of 1917. You can see the Vimy Memorial and will pass by Vimy village (on your left). The road climbs the Ridge and you will pass Thelus and drive across the famous Canadian Battlefield of April 9th, 1917. Follow the road into Arras.

View of Lens from the Green Crassier. (Christie)

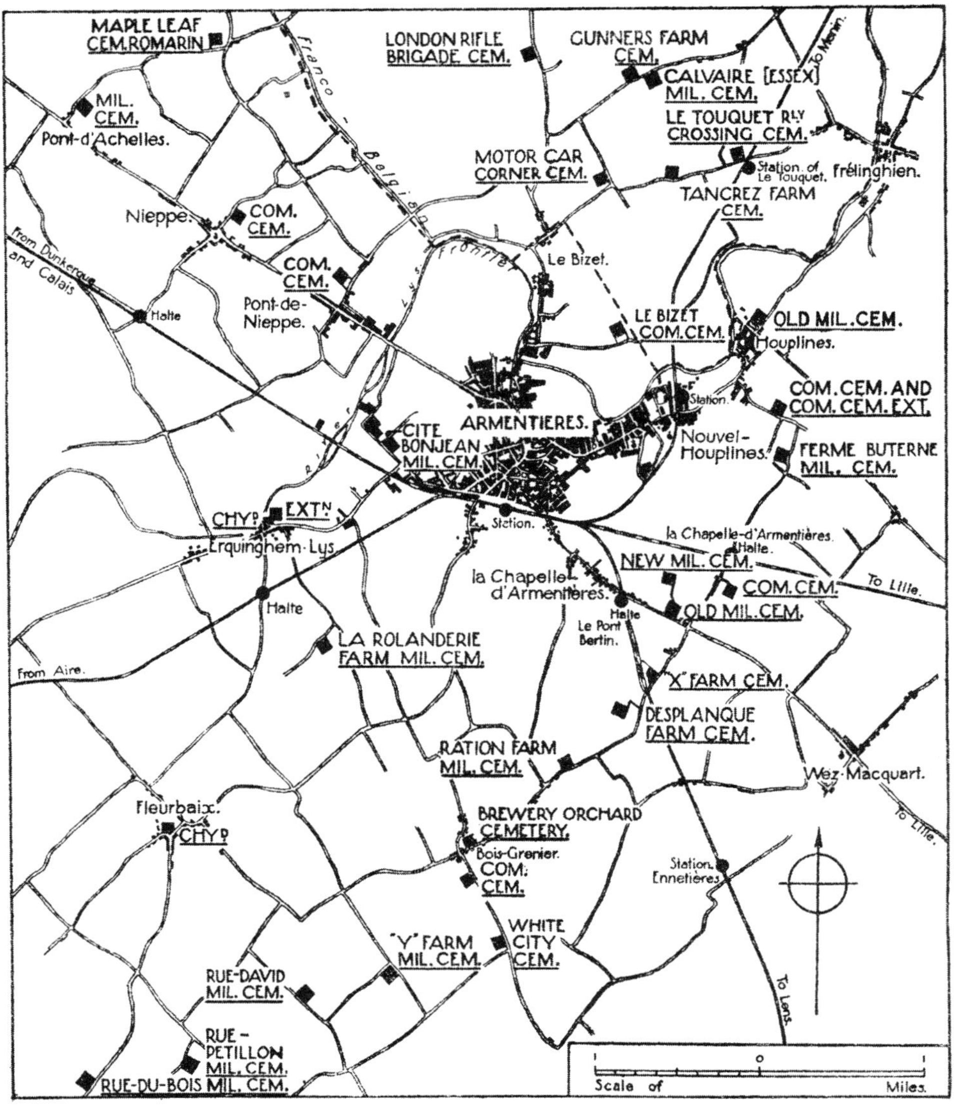

Cemeteries in the Armentieres Sector.

Cemeteries and Memorials

Fleurbaix - Festubert - Givenchy - Hill 70

Eighty percent of the Canadians who lost their lives in the Battles of Festubert and Givenchy have no known grave and are commemorated on The Vimy Memorial to the Missing. Only a handful are buried in known graves. Roughly 60% of those killed in the Battle of Hill 70 have no known grave and are commemorated on Vimy Ridge. The rest lie in the many cemeteries in the Lens-Arras region. The main cemeteries are listed below:

Le Trou Aid Post Cemetery, Fleurbaix

Le Trou Aid Post Cemetery is located three km NW of the village of Fromelles on the D22c. The Cemetery was first used in October 1914 and was used until July 1915 when it contained 123 graves. After the war 230 graves were brought into the cemetery from the surrounding battlefields. It now contains 351 Commonwealth burials, including 7 Canadians. Six of the Canadians were members of the 14th Canadian Infantry Battalion killed in early March 1915.

Brigadier General Arthur Lowry-Cole of the 25th Imperial Brigade died of wounds received at Aubers Ridge, May 9th, 1915. He is buried in E.22. This cemetery is one of the most beautiful in France. It is built on an island and is surrounded by Weeping Willows.

Rue Petillon Military Cemetery, Fleurbaix

Rue Petillon Military Cemetery is three km north of Fromelles on the D175. The cemetery was used by fighting units from December 1914 until April 1918. It was enlarged after the war by the concentration of 859 graves from the surrounding battlefields. It now contains 1,507 Commonwealth burials including 55 Canadians (17 are unidentified).

The 20 original Canadian burials belong to Battalions in the 3rd Canadian Infantry Brigade killed on the Fleurbaix Sector in March 1915. Fifteen Canadians are commemorated by Special Memorials. They were killed at Hill 70 on August 15th, 1917 and buried in Eighth Canadian Cemetery, Lens. The cemetery was obliterated in later fighting and the graves could not be found after the war. There is a special stone, known as a Duhallow Block, in front of their headstones, giving the details of the lost graves. As with all Special Memorials (those that do not mark a grave), they are located along the wall of the cemetery and not in a Burial Plot. They usually have Kipling's inscription *"Their Glory Shall Not Be Blotted Out"* engraved at the bottom of their headstones. They are also known as "Kiplings."

The other Canadian graves were brought in from the Lens-Hill 70 Battlefields, with the exception of Arthur Young of the 46th Battalion whose remains were found on Vimy Ridge in 1922.

There are 292 (22 are unidentified) Australians buried in the cemetery. The majority were killed at Fromelles..

Rue David Military Cemetery, Fleurbaix

Rue David Military Cemetery is four km north of Fromelles on the D176. It was used by fighting units from October 1914 until December 1917. It was enlarged after the war by the concentration of 656 graves from the surrounding battlefields. It now contains 893 Commonwealth burials, including 10 Canadians (all are identified).

The Canadian burials belong to men of the 2nd Infantry Brigade who were killed in early March 1915. They are not original burials. Six were brought in from Abbey Wall Cemetery, LaBoutilliere. Amongst those brought in from Abbey Wall was Major Percy Rigby of the 7th Canadian Infantry. He had served in the Sherwood Foresters from 1900-1911, been twice Mentioned in Despatches in the Boer War, and commanded the 4th King's African Rifles from 1905-1907. This professional soldier was ranching at Fernie, BC when he enlisted in the CEF in 1914. The History of the 7th Battalion states, "Rigby was quite the most experienced officer in the Regiment. His mild eccentricities appealed to all and everyone had the greatest confidence in his ability as a leader." Percy Rigby was killed in action March 10th, 1915, age 43 years (II. D.49.).

Y Farm Military Cemetery, Fleurbaix

Y Farm Military Cemetery is located four km north of Fromelles on the D176, 500 metres east of Rue David Cemetery. It was used by fighting units from March 1915 until February 1918. It was expanded by 335 graves by battlefield clearances after the war. It now contains 819 Commonwealth burials, including 24 Canadians (two, brought in from the Vimy battlefield in 1923, are unidentified).

Eby, Private Alexander Ralph; 5th Battalion, C.E.F.; eldest son of Alexander Eby of Berlin, Ontario; great great grandson of Bishop Benjamin Eby, of the Mennonite Connection, who founded the town of Berlin; born Berlin, Ontario, 3 Aug. 1891; educated at Berlin Public and High Schools; in 1908 homesteaded in Abbey, Saskatchewan; on outbreak of war enlisted at Swift Current; went overseas in Oct. 1914; to France with the First Contingent in Feb. 1915; was killed there 21 March 1915; unmarried. Major G.S. Pragnell wrote, "He was one of the best and most willing men of the company and at the time he was actually shot he was working hard to strengthen the trench," and later Lieut. L.F. Page: "Ever since your brother came under my commission at Valcartier I always found him most cheerful and willing. He was making a good soldier and always doing his duty well." three of his comrades wrote: "your brother's death was severely felt by the remainder of the boys of his company as he was a general favourite with all who knew him. He was buried at La Boutillerie Chateau, a few miles east of Laventie, in the evening of March 21, by the chaplain of our Battn., beside two of his comrades." His remains were moved to Rue David Military Cemetery in 1920, and he still rests beside his comrades, Privates Beames and Proven, in grave III. A.44.

Hopey, Private Edmund Eugene; 14th Battalion, C.E.F.; only child of George Allen Hopey of Dorchester, Mass., U.S.A.; educated there; was a carpenter by trade; joined the Massachusetts Militia 1914; on the outbreak of war went to St. John, N.B., and enlisted in the 14th Battn.; went overseas in Oct. 1914, and to France on 7 Feb. 1915, and was killed in action near Fleurbaix, 4 March 1915; unmarried. He was buried in Le Trou Aid Post (J.2.). Captain Curry of the 14th Battn. wrote to his mother, speaking highly of his bravery. He met his death while covering the parapet.

Twenty-one burials belong to Canadians of the 1st Infantry Brigade killed in March 1915. They are buried in Rows H and J. The remains of Private Kenneth Spencer, 13th Battalion (Black Watch) were brought into the cemetery from an isolated grave in 1923. Spencer was killed in action on February 27th, 1915.

Captain John Manuel, DSC, of 210 Squadron RAF, is buried in N.7. Manuel was an Ace with 9 kills, including 7 Albatros DVs. On June 10th, 1918 he was on a fighting patrol over the lines at Laventie when his Sopwith Camel collided with another Camel when diving on an Enemy Aircraft. He was from Edmonton, Alberta. The Pilot of the other plane, Second Lieutenant F.C. Dodd, is buried in N.6. For CWGC statistical purposes all RAF casualties are counted as British, so Manuel is not counted as a Canadian in the cemetery records.

Lieutenant George Moor, VC, MC & Bar of the 2nd Hampshire Regiment won his Victoria Cross during the infamous Third Battle of Krithia in Gallipoli on June 5th, 1915. He died November 3rd, 1918 and is buried in C.86.

Sailly-sur-la-Lys Canadian Cemetery

Sailly-sur-la-Lys Canadian Cemetery is located on the D945 just west of Sailly, 8 km NW of Fromelles. There are two cemeteries here, Anzac on the north side of the road and Sailly Canadian on the south side. The cemetery was started by the Canadians in March 1915 and used by fighting units until July 1916. It contains 313 Commonwealth burials including 9 Canadians.

The 9 Canadians were all killed in March 1915 and are from all three Brigades of the 1st Canadian Division. One of the Canadians served under an alias. Private Adrian Vuilleumier of the 10th Canadian Battalion, was killed March 17th, 1915 (III.B.16.). He was working as a tradesman in Calgary when he enlisted in 1914. After his death, it was determined his true name was Jules Schmidt and he was from Mulhouse, France. One can speculate he changed his names because it was too Germanic for the CEF. Schmidt has the "*J. Schmidt served as*" inscription on his headstone.

Le Touret Military Cemetery, Richebourg-L'Avoue

Le Touret Military Cemetery is located four km west of Neuve Chapelle on the D171. The cemetery was started in November 1914 and used by fighting units until March 1918. The cemetery now contains 911 Commonwealth burials including 11 Canadians. At the end of the war there were 264 Portugese graves, but they were later removed.

The Canadians buried here were all killed at Festubert. Seven are members of the 5th Canadian Infantry Battalion, and include Major Daniel Tenaille, Captain James Innes-Hopkins and Lieutenant James Currie. All three are mentioned in Harold Baldwin's memoir, "*Holding The Line*", published in1918. They are buried in II.C.13, B.15 and B.16 respectively.

There are six British or Indian Army Lieutenant-Colonels in the cemetery, as well as Gurkha officers, all killed in 1914-15. In 1925 they were rebuilding the estaminet, La Bombe, opposite the Indian Memorial, when the mother of a missing officer appeared stating she knew he was there. After some searching they found his lost remains. Second Lieutenant Cyril Crichton, killed March 10th, 1915 is now buried in IV.C.34. (See *Thirteen Years After* by Will R. Bird, CEF Books, 2001.)

The Le Touret Memorial to the Missing is at the east end of the cemetery, and lists 13,373 British soldiers missing in the fighting in this area (La Bassee, Neuve Chapelle, Aubers, Festubert and Givenchy) from October 1914 until September 24th, 1915. The Indians (Undivided India) and Canadians missing in these actions are commemorated at Neuve Chapelle and Vimy.

Brown's Road Military Cemetery, Festubert

Brown's Road Military Cemetery is located one km SW of Festubert, just off the D166. It was started in October 1914 and used until November 1917. After the war it was enlarged by the concentration of 742 graves from the surrounding battlefields. It now contains 1,068 Commonwealth burials, including 21 Canadians (three are unidentified).

Nine of the identified Canadians buried here were killed in the Battle of Festubert. They are all members of the 10th Canadian Infantry killed May 21st, 1915. The others were killed or died of wounds shortly after the battle ended.

Guard's Cemetery (Windy Corner), Cuinchy

Guards Cemetery is located two km south of Festubert just off the D166. It was started in January 1915 at Windy Corner, so called due to German machine-gunners constantly shooting at the crossroads, and was used until May 1916. It was greatly enlarged after the war by the concentration of 2,720 graves from the surrounding battlefields. It now contains 3,407 Commonwealth burials (65% are unidentified), including 32 Canadians (one is unidentified).

All the Canadians in the cemetery were killed in the Battle of Festubert, and were concentrated into the cemetery. Nine of the Canadians belong to the 14th Canadian Infantry and were killed May 20th-21st, 1915. Seven others were members of the 8th Battalion killed on the same date.

Lieutenant Robin Johnston, a Canadian from New Brunswick, in No. 2 Squadron, RAF, is buried in VII.J.44. His two-seater was shot down on May 9th, 1918. Oddly his observer, Albert Melanson, also a Canadian, has no known grave and is commemorated on the Air Services Memorial at Arras.

There is one Victoria Cross winner in the cemetery, Major John Mackenzie, VC, was killed at Festubert on May 17th, 1915 with the 1st Bedfords. He won his VC in the Ashanti Campaign in 1900 (VIII. J.10.). A British Brigadier General with the most amazing name is buried here. The Honourable John Hepburn-Stuart-Forbes-Trefusis, DSO, of the Irish Guards, was killed in action October 24th, 1915 (III. J.4.)

Beauvry Communal Cemetery

Beauvry is a village three km SE of Bethune. The Communal Cemetery is in the west end of the village. It was used from 1914-16 and contains 68 Commonwealth graves, including 7 Canadians. They are buried in rows in the midst of the civilian graves.

The Canadian graves are all officers killed at Givenchy in June 1915. Five belong to the 1st Battalion, including their Commanding Officer, Lieutenant-Colonel Henry Becher and three Captains, Peter Pick, Frederic Robinson, George Smith and Lieutenant Cecil James. They were all killed June 15th, 1915.

Bethune Town Cemetery

Bethune Town Cemetery is located in the NE part of the town, on the road to Estaires (D945). Bethune was an important transport and medical hub throughout the war. The first British burials in the cemetery date from November 1914, and the last burials were in the Fall of 1918. It now contains 3,004 Commonwealth graves, including 55 Canadians.

Beauvry Cemetery. (Christie)

The grave of Lt. Col. H.C. Becher. (Christie)

Lieut.-Col. H. C. Becher, 1st Battalion West Ontario Regiment (killed).

Twenty-nine of the Canadians died of wounds received in the Battle of Festubert, one from Givenchy, and 18 from the Battle of Hill 70.

Lieutenant Frank DePass, VC, of the 34th Poona Horse is buried in I.A.24. DePass won his VC posthumously when attacking a German trench and rescuing a wounded soldier near Festubert on November 24th, 1915.

There are two British Brigadiers in the cemetery. Godfrey Matthews, RMLI, died of wounds April 13th, 1917. He was commanding the 198th British Brigade (III. K. 56.). Previously he had been the Governor of the Upper Nile (1903-1909). George Nugent, Irish Guards, was commanding the 141st British Brigade, when he was killed in action at Givenchy on May 31st, 1915 (II.J.1.). There are also 9 British Lieutenant-Colonels buried in the cemetery.

There are 19 Second World War burials in the cemetery, including two Canadians.

Hinges Military Cemetery

Hinges Military Cemetery is located five km NE of Bethune on the D180, SE of Hinges village. It was used by Field Ambulances from May to August 1915. It now contains 101 Commonwealth graves, including 26 Canadians (all are identified). All the Canadians died of wounds received in the Battle of Festubert.

Colonel George Naismith of the CAMC visited the cemetery after the battle, and he wrote of his visit in his 1917 book, *"On The Fringe of The Great Fight,"* "... one of our field ambulances had been located in the spacious shady grounds of the chateau. A little graveyard near the main gateway, on the roadside, is the last sleeping place of a number of Canadians who died in this ambulance. Today a neat fence surrounds this little area of Canadian soil and the graves are kept trim and covered with flowers... I saw the French country people themselves decorating the little mounds beneath which lay "Les Canadiens" who had come so far to fight for France in this struggle for the freedom of the world. It is a beautiful little sleeping place, and somehow it never seemed so sad a spot as some of the other graveyards in France where our Canadians lie... when the sky flickered red as from summer lightening with the flash of a myriad of shells, and the horizon was defined in electric green from the flares of the Germans, I fancied I could see the shadowy spirits of the departed ones hovering over this spot."

Brown, Private Edward, 8th Battn., C.E.F.; third son of George and Louisa Brown of Lloydminster, Saskatchewan; born Yorkshire, 5 Aug. 1888; went to Canada with the Barr Family of Colonists in 1903; he volunteered in Nov. 1914; and went to the front 26/27 April 1915; was seriously wounded on the night of 20/21 May at Festubert, and died on 23 May. Buried at Hinges, A.10.

Ellis, Private Judson Harold, 3rd Field Ambulance, C.A.M.C.; eldest son of William and Elizabeth Ellis of Alliston, Ontario; born Thornbury, Ontario 24 March 1891; enlisted Aug. 1914; went to France Feb. 1915; died 21 May 1915, of wounds received while attending to the wounded at Festubert; unmarried. He is buried at Hinges, A.1.

Hazel, Private John Thomas, 5th Battn., C.E.F.; son of William and Mary Hazel of Middlesbrough, England; born there 13 Jan. 1891; went to Canada to farm in 1908; volunteered on the outbreak of war; went to France Feb. 1915; died of wounds 26 May 1915, received at Festubert; unmarried. He is buried at Hinges, A.19.

Denny, Private Robert Edmund Barry, 16th Battn., Canadian Scottish, C.E.F.; 2nd son of Edmund and Emily Denny of Lincolnshire, England; born Wragby, England 19 March 1891; educated Sutton Valence School, Kent; went to Canada in May 1913; enlisted with his brother on the outbreak of war; went overseas in Oct. 1914, and to France in Feb. 1915. He came safely through the charge at Kitchener's Wood, but was seriously wounded by a shell while on patrol at Festubert, and died in hospital at Bethune, 22 May 1915, having been recommended for a commission a few days previously. He is buried in Bethune Town Cemetery, IV.C.49.; unmarried. One comrade wrote of him: "He was one of the most courageous of comrades and I have seen him perform several deeds worthy of recognition"; and another: "He was wounded doing his duty as a soldier should, and evidences of his coolness and bravery under heavy fire were numerous. I once assisted him to bandage a wounded comrade. The King has lost a good soldier, and we a good pal." His three brothers also served.

Morrison, Captain Thomas Edmund, Canadian Engineers; eldest son of Joseph Morrison of Montreal; born Montreal, 10 July 1887; educated Royal Military College, Kingston, graduated 1908; gazetted 2nd. Lieut. Royal Canadian Engineers, 1908; Captain, 1913; on outbreak of war was sent to Valcartier; sailed overseas Oct. 1914; 8 Feb. 1915 went to France. He took part in many engagements, including Second Battle of Ypres, and the Battle of Festubert, and was killed in action at Givenchy, 15 June 1915. An officer writing of him, spoke highly of his work, saying how he worked night and day in the trenches ahead of the British force, exposed all the time to the enemy fire. He married at Toronto, 8 Aug. 1914, Ethel Frederica Clare. Buried in Bethune Town Cemetery, II.J.2.

Chocques Military Cemetery

Chocques Military Cemetery is located five km west of Bethune, in the northern side of the village (D181). The cemetery was first used in January 1915 and used by Casualty Clearing Stations until September 1918. After the war 90 graves were brought in from smaller cemeteries. It now contains 1,737 Commonwealth burials, including 51 Canadians.

Nineteen of the Canadian graves belong to men who died of wounds received at Festubert, and 15 burials are those mortally wounded at Hill 70.

Second Lieutenant Alexander Turner, VC won a posthumous VC for bravery at Vermelles on September 28th, 1915. He died of wounds received in this action (I. B.2.) His bother, Victor Turner, won the VC in North Africa in 1942. The Reverend Oswin Creighton, Chaplain to the Forces, was killed in action April 15th, 1918. He had served in Gallipoli and had written a memoir on his experiences, "*With The Twenty-Ninth Division in Gallipoli*, 1916." He is buried in I.P.34.

Lillers Communal Cemetery

Lillers is 15 km west of Bethune. Lillers Communal Cemetery is in the northern end of the village beside the Nave River, on the road to St. Venant (D916). It was used by Casualty Clearing Stations throughout the war. The cemetery contains 894 Commonwealth burials, including 42 Canadians.

The Canadians buried reflect the Battles of Festubert (8), Givenchy (7) and Hill 70 (9).

There are two Victoria Cross winners buried in the Cemetery. Major David Nelson, VC of the RFA, was a member of the famous "L" Battery, and won his VC, September 1st, 1914. He died of wounds April 8th, 1918 (V.A.16.). Corporal William Cotter, VC, of The Buffs, won a posthumous VC for incredible bravery. His Citation reads, "*When his right leg had been blown off at the knee and he had also been wounded in both arms, he made his way unaided for fifty yards... steadied the men... controlled their fire, issued orders and altered dispositions of his men to meet a fresh counter-attack... For two hours he held his position... He could not be moved back for fourteen hours.*" He died 8 days later, March 14th, 1916 (IV.E.45.).

Loos British Cemetery

Loos is a village three km NW of Lens. It was captured by the British in the Battle of Loos, September 25th, 1915. The cemetery is on the south side of the village. It was started by the Canadian Corps in July 1917, and the original burials are in Plot I, Rows A and B, and Plot II, Row A. After the war 2,758 graves were brought into the cemetery from the surrounding battlefields, and from several small cemeteries. Of the 2,175 isolated graves brought into the cemetery from the 1915 Loos battlefield, 90% are unidentified. It now contains 2,847 Commonwealth burials, including 445 Canadians (204 are unidentified).

Of the identified Canadian burials 129 are those killed at Hill 70. Ninety-five belong to men of the 1st Division and 44 to the 2nd Division.

One of the cemeteries concentrated into Loos in 1925 was Corkscrew Cemetery (44A M11 a3.3). During the relocation Anna Durie of Toronto stole the body of her son, Captain William Durie, and took him back to Canada for reburial. This was against War Graves policy but Mrs. Durie and her French operatives were so shrewd that the CWGC did not find out about it until notice of his reburial appeared in Toronto newspapers. Durie was originally buried in XX. G. 15. (See *The Canadians at Passchendaele, For King & Empire, Volume IV*, CEF Books, Revised 2007.)

Private Chikara Fujita of Kakura, Japan was killed at Hill 70 serving with the 10th Canadian Infantry (III. A. 3.). Fujita was one of 250 Japanese-Canadians who fought with the CEF, of whom one third were killed. The Japanese, who resided in British Columbia were not allowed to enlist there, so they crossed the Rockies and enlisted in Alberta or Saskatchewan. They fought well for Canada and felt their sacrifice would be awarded with full Citizenship. They were to be disappointed. Sadly some of the Japanese veterans were interned by the Canadian Government in the Second World War.

Lieven Communal Cemetery Extension

The cemetery is located in the southwest side of the old mining town of Lievin, three km west of Lens. The cemetery was made after the war by the concentration of ten smaller cemeteries and from isolated remains found on the old Vimy-Lens battlefield. It now contains 676 Commonwealth graves, including153 Canadians (56 are unidentified).

Japanese soldiers in the 10th (Alberta) Battalion, July 1917. Otokichi Onishi (back row, left), Chikara Fujita (middle 2nd left), and Toraki Matsumura (middle, 2nd right) were all killed in the Battle of Hill 70. Fujita is buried in Loos.

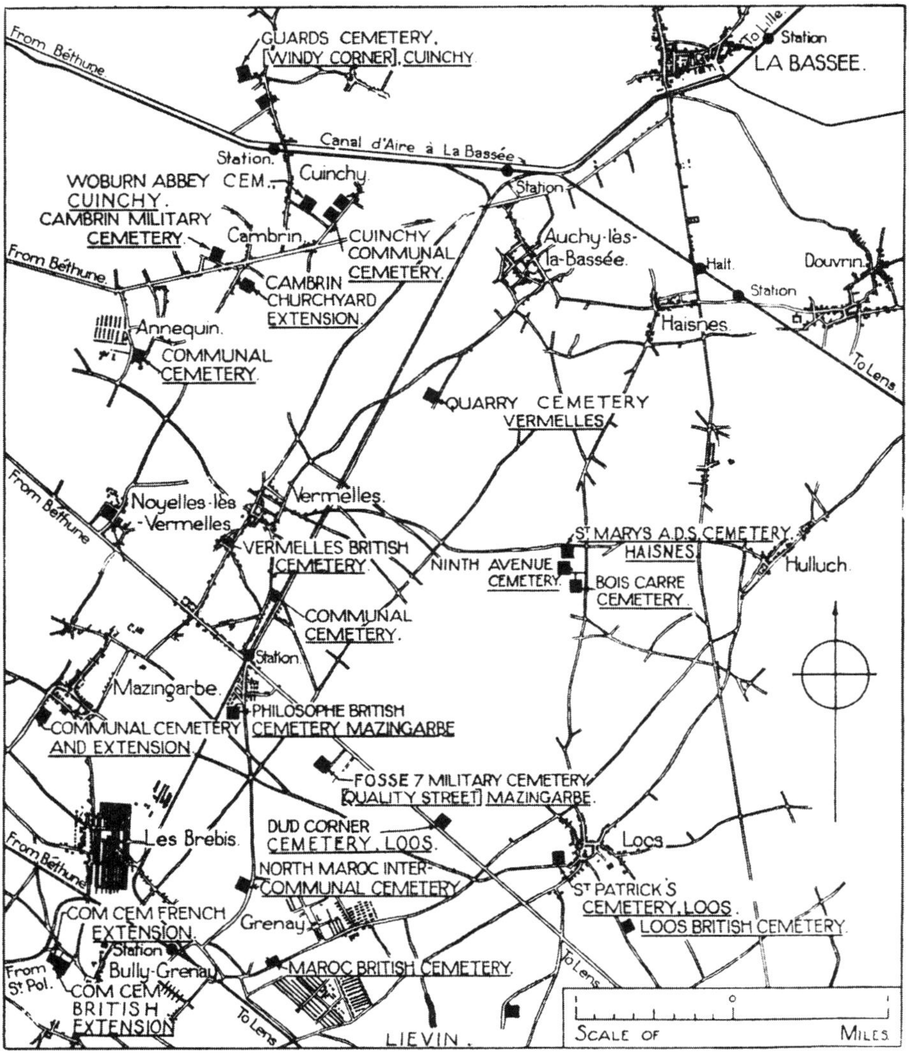

Cemeteries near Hill 70.

Forty of the Canadian burials are those of men killed in the Battle of Vimy Ridge, and 40 are those killed in the fighting in Lens in August 1917. The graves from the Lens fighting are almost exclusively from the 4th Division, predominantly men from the 75th (12), 87th (4) and 102nd (4) Battalions.

Maroc British Cemetery, Grenay

Grenay is a village three km west of Loos. Maroc British Cemetery is on the east side of the village on the road to Loos (D165). The cemetery was started by the French in 1915, and taken over by British units in January 1916. It was enlarged after the war by the concentration of 340 graves found on the old battlefields or buried in smaller cemeteries. It now contains 1,290 Commonwealth graves, including 178 Canadians (14 are unidentified).

The Canadians buried here were killed in the many trench raids that took place near here in 1917 and from the constant stream of casualties from holding the line. In addition there are 46 graves of Canadian soldiers who died of wounds received in the Battle of Hill 70. The majority belong to the 1st Division.

Bully Grenay Communal Cemetery British Extension

Bully Grenay is a village five km west of Loos. The Cemetery is two km west of Maroc British, and is in the centre of the village. The British Extension was started in April 1916, and used until October 1918. After the war it was enlarged by the concentration of 168 graves from the surrounding region. It now contains 765 Commonwealth burials, including 172 Canadians (three are unidentified).

The majority buried here reflect the high level of activity in the Lens Sector, the trench raids (particularly August 9th, 1917 and March 4th, 1918), and daily losses known as "trench wastage." There are 15 men of the 1st Heavy Battery, Canadian Garrison Artillery, buried in Plot III. Row E, who were killed when a shell exploded prematurely in the barrel of their 60 pounder gun on August 9th, 1917.

There are also graves of 18 men who died in the Battle of Hill 70 in the cemetery.

Mazingarbe Communal Cemetery & Extension

Mazingarge is a village six km west of Loos. The cemetery is on the

SW side of the village on the road to Sains-en-Gohelle (D75). The Extension was started in April 1916 and used until October 1918. It contains 356 Commonwealth graves, including 66 Canadians (all are identified).

Twenty-nine of the Canadian graves are those who died in the Battle of Hill 70, the majority belong to men of the 1st Division. Most of the other Canadian burials belong to men killed holding the line in the winter of 1917-18.

Fosse No.10 Communal Cemetery Extension, Sains-en-Gohelle

Sains-en-Gohelle is a village 8 km west of Loos. The Cemetery is located on the south side of the village. Fosse No.10 was a pithead and a collection of miners' houses during the war. The Extension was started in April 1916 and was used mainly by Field Ambulances until October 1918. It contains 467 Commonwealth graves, including 214 Canadians (all are identified). There are also the graves of 49 members of the Chinese Labour Corps in the cemetery. Many of these men were recruited in Canada.

The Canadian graves cover the period from the summer of 1917 until mid-1918. There are 30 graves of Canadian soldiers killed in the Battle of Hill 70.

Private Charles Kerr, of Fox River, NS, serving with the 49th Canadian Infantry, was killed in action December 28th, 1917. He is buried in III.C.2. His brother, John Chipman Kerr, won the Victoria Cross also with the 49th during the Battle of the Somme in 1916.

Aix Noulette Communal Cemetery Extension

Aix-Noulette is a village 12 km north of Arras on the road to Bethune(937). The Extension is just east of the village on the road to Bully-les-Mines. The Extension was started by French troops in 1915, was taken over by British troops in February 1916 and was used until October 1918. Sixty-three graves were brought in from the surrounding region after the war. It now contains 749 Commonwealth burials, including 492 Canadians (10 are unidentified).

The Canadian burials date from spring 1917 through to the winter of 1918. There are 162 graves of Canadians who died in the Battle of Hill 70, mostly 2nd and 4th Divisions. The cemetery also illustrates the heavy price paid by the Canadians in holding the Vimy-Lens Sector. The majority of the men buried here died in day-to-day operations, not in major attacks.

The Rippingale brothers, Benjamin and Stanley, of Peterborough, were both killed on July 16th, 1917 when a German rifle grenade hit their Lewis Gun position. They were serving with the 20th Canadian Infantry, and are buried in I. G. 11 and 12 respectively.

Private Horace Stokes of Brantford, Ontario, enlisted two weeks after his son, Stanley, at Brantford. Horace was killed in action September 19th, 1917, serving with the 1st Canadian Infantry (I.T.2.). Stanley, also with the 1st was killed in action at Vimy Ridge, and is buried at Ecoivres Military Cemetery (VI.E.3.). Stanley was only fourteen years old when he enlisted.

Noeux-les-Mines Communal Cemetery & Extension

Noeux-les-Mines is a town 24 km north of Arras on the D937. The cemetery is on the NE side of the town. Both the Communal Cemetery and the Extension are located in the Civilian cemetery. The Communal Cemetery was first used in June 1915. It was filled by August 1917 when the Extension was first used, the last burials there being made in December 1918. It now contains 1,285 Commonwealth graves, including 297 Canadians. Roughly 200 graves are of British soldiers who died in the Battle of Loos, 1915.

The Canadian burials originate from the summer of 1917 when the Canadian Corps moved north from Vimy in anticipation of the Battle of Hill 70. Seventy-nine burials are those of Canadians who died at Hill 70. It is the only Cemetery that contains two Canadian VC winners, both were posthumous awards from Hill 70. Private Harry Brown, VC, of the 10th Canadian Infantry (Alberta), won an epic VC for acting as a runner under the most dangerous conditions. Brown delivered his message but not before he was mortally wounded (II.J.29.). Major Okill Learmonth, VC, MC, of the 2nd Canadian Infantry, played a critical role in driving back many German counter-attacks. Although mortally wounded he continued to inspire his men, and even threw back German grenades (II.K.9.).

Private H.E.J. Lodge, of the 19th Canadian Infantry, was one of 25 Canadians executed in the war. Lodge was shot for desertion on March 13th, 1918 (Extension IV.B. 5.).

There are two British Generals buried in the Communal Cemetery:

Major-General F.D. Wing of the Royal Field Artillery, was killed in action at Loos, October 2nd, 1915 (I.K.15.), and Brigadier General Malcolm Peake, also of the RFA, was killed in action August 27th, 1917 (I.U.2.).

Barlin Communal Cemetery Extension

The cemetery is north of the village of Barlin, which is 10 km east of Béthune. The cemetery was established by the French in 1914 and subsequently taken over by British and Canadian Casualty Clearing Stations.

It now contains the graves of 1,095 Commonwealth soldiers including 677 Canadians. More than 200 burials are Canadians mortally wounded in the capture of Vimy Ridge. Many of the others died of wounds received holding the line in front of Vimy or on the Douai Plain later in the year. Fifty graves belong to men who died of wounds received during the Battle of Hill 70 in August 1917.

Buried in Plot I, Row J, Grave 50 is Lieutenant Alfred Norsworthy of the 73rd Battalion (Black Watch of Montreal). Norsworthy died of wounds March 29th, 1917. His older brother, Major Edward Norsworthy, was killed while on active service with the 13th Battalion (Black Watch of Montreal). On April 22nd, 1915, Major Norsworthy's courageous action against the Germans on the Canadians' open flank helped save the day during the poison gas attack (see *For King & Empire; Volume I; The Canadians at Ypres, April, 1915*).

Company Quarter Master Sergeant William Alexander has the unfortunate claim of being the highest ranking Canadian executed during the war. Alexander had served at the front since February 1915 without running afoul of the military authorities. He deserted during the Battle of Hill 70, and was recaptured shortly after and tried for Desertion. In spite of his clean record nothing could save him from the firing squad, including a last-minute effort by the Chaplain of the 1st Canadian Division, Frederick Scott. The highly-respected Padre appealed to Alexander's Commanders but to no avail. He was shot on October 18th, 1917. His case was one of the most tragic of the war as it seemed so blatantly unfair. Canon Scott wrote of that awful night in his memoir *The Great War As I Saw It* (CEF Books, 2000).

Alexander's family in Winnipeg was torn apart by his shocking death and wrote; "May the Lord have Mercy on the man who judged him, if he was wrong." CQMS Alexander is buried in Plot II, Row D, Grave 43.

Lieutenant Geoffrey Brichta, of Sutton West, Ontario, was the observer in a two-seater, BE2c, which was shot down over Souchez by Manfred von Richthofen on March 6th, 1917. Brichta and his pilot, Second Lieutenant Gerald Gossett-Bibby, were the Red Baron's 24th Kill. They are buried in I. J.53-54. In the Second World War Brichta's son, Philip, enlisted in the RCAF. He was killed in action when his Wellington bomber was shot down over Germany, September 16th, 1942, and is buried in Reichwald War Cemetery, Germany, Collective Grave 23.A.7-9. Philip was 31 when he died, a year younger than his father when he was killed on the Western Front.

Lapugnoy Military Cemetery

The cemetery is northwest of the village of Lapugnoy (six km west of Béthune). It was established in 1915 and used for burials from nearby Casualty Clearing Stations. It now contains 1,319 Commonwealth graves (including more than 150 British soldiers killed in the Battle of Loos, September 1915), 349 of them are Canadian (one unknown).

One hundred and thirty-three of the Canadians buried here were wounded in the Battles of Vimy Ridge, Arleux and Fresnoy. Another 49 succumbed to their wounds received in the Battle of Hill 70. Canadian units also buried their dead here in 1918. For 18 months this area was an operational centre for the Canadian operations on the Vimy front.

Victor Wheeler, a Signaller in the 50th (Alberta) Battalion, wrote a powerful memoir of his experiences on the Western Front. Wheeler's heart-felt memoir, *The 50th Battalion in No Man's Land* (CEF Books, 2000), recounts life with his closest friends, the Waller brothers, Art, Harry and Robert of Calgary, Alberta. During the attack on the Pimple, Harry was severely wounded by an explosion when entering a German dugout. Barely alive and almost cut in two, Harry rested in his brother Art's arms, until he was stretchered away. He died 5 days later. Art was killed a year later. Robert survived the war. Harry Waller is buried in Plot III, Row A, Grave 13.

Bruay Communal Cemetery Extension

The cemetery is located northwest of the old coal mining village of Bruay, which is five km west of Béthune. Set amongst the monumental slag heaps, it was established by French troops in October 1914 and used by British and Canadian units from 1916 to 1918. It contains the graves of 412 Commonwealth soldiers of which 276 are Canadian.

Sixty-three of the Canadian burials belong to those who died of wounds received in the Battle of Vimy Ridge. The rest of the Canadian graves are those mortally wounded while holding the line through 1917 or in the Battle of Hill 70 (24).

Cabaret Rouge British Cemetery, Souchez

Cabaret Rouge is one km south of Souchez on the main Arras-Béthune road. Souchez is 11 km north of Arras. The cemetery was established in 1916 and used until the end of the war. The original burials are in Plots I through V (the plots far right of the Stone of Remembrance). Battlefield clearances between 1922 and 1927 brought in more than 7,000 burials from areas as far south as Amiens and as far north as Armentières on the Belgian border. It now contains the graves of 7,645 Commonwealth soldiers (59% are unidentified), of which 741 are Canadian (422 are unidentified).

Many are men of the 3rd and 4th Canadian Divisions killed at the Battle of Vimy Ridge. They are buried in the plots surrounding the Stone of Remembrance.

The other Canadian burials are related to many battles. There are 20 graves of Canadians killed at Givenchy. They were found in a trench on the edge of Red Dragon Crater in 1923. Eleven were identified (XVII. Rows E and F). Another 30 were recovered from the Hill 70/Lens battlefield. The majority of the burials are from Vimy and the actions near Lens and Avion in May and June 1917. Some men killed in the March 1st, 1917 trench raid are also buried here, most of them unidentified.

This spectacular cemetery contains burials that trace the history of the British Expeditionary Force on the Western Front, 1914-1918. There are many graves of regular British and Indian Army men killed during the Race to the Sea in 1914, the Battles of Neuve Chapelle and Aubers Ridge in 1915, Vimy Ridge in 1916-17 and the Battle of the Lys in 1918. There are also numerous Royal Flying Corps pilots who were killed behind the German lines and whose remains were brought here after the war.

Of interest are the graves of two brothers. Buried in Plot XII, Row E, Graves 16 and 15, Privates Olivier and Wilfred Chenier of the Royal Canadian Regiment, sons of Janvier Olivier, were killed on the same day, April 9th, 1917. They were aged 27 and 28 respectively.

Lieutenant Frederick G. Scott, Canadian Field Artillery, is buried in Plot XV, Row M, Grave19. Scott was a good friend of Conn Smythe, founder/owner of the Toronto Maple Leafs. Scott's sad death had an enormous influence on Smythe and was recounted in his autobiography, *If You Can't Beat 'Em in the Alley.*

In May 2000 the Canadian Government exhumed an Unknown Canadian Soldier and repatriated him to Canada, where he was re-interred as Canada's Unknown Soldier in Ottawa. The body was taken from Plot VIII, Row E, Grave 7. During the battlefield clearances a trench burial containing more than 20 members of the 87th (Canadian Grenadier Guards) Battalion, all killed on the morning of April 9th, 1917, was moved to Cabaret Rouge. Canada's Unknown soldier is one of these men. His identity cannot be confirmed but he is one of 20 or so 87th men who have no known grave and are commemorated on the Vimy Memorial. In place of his old headstone a commemorative marker has been erected. It states:

THE FORMER GRAVE OF AN
UNKNOWN CANADIAN SOLDIER
OF THE FIRST WORLD WAR.
HIS REMAINS WERE REMOVED
ON 29 MAY 2000 AND NOW
LIE INTERRED AT THE
NATIONAL WAR MEMORIAL
IN OTTAWA, CANADA.

From the northern side of the cemetery there is an excellent view of the Notre-Dame de Lorette French National Memorial.

Hospital Centres

Longuenesse (Souvenir) Cemetery, St. Omer

St. Omer is a large town 60 km NW of Arras on the N43. It was an important transport, supply and medical centre throughout the war. The cemetery is located SW of the town, near the hamlet of Longuesse. It contains 2,769 Commonwealth burials, including 148 Canadians (all are identified).

The Canadian graves date from early 1915 until the end of 1918. There are five burials of Canadians who died of wounds received in the Fleurbaix Sector, 11 graves of men mortally wounded at Festubert, and 31 graves of Canadian soldiers who were mortally wounded at Hill 70. There are also 11 graves of Canadians who served with the Royal Flying Corps or the Royal Air Force.

The cemetery contains one VC winner, Lance Corporal Cecil Noble, VC, of the Rifle Brigade, who won his VC posthumously for bravery at Neuve Chapelle on March 12th, 1915 (I.A.57.). There are two British Nurses and two VADs buried in VI. B.1- 4., who were killed in a German air raid on the hospitals on September 30th, 1917.

It is a very interesting cemetery and contains burials from many unusual units such as; the Chinese Labour Corps (64), Indian Army (5), South African Native Labour Corps (5 Zulus), and soldiers from the British West Indies Regiment (12).

There are 403 Second World War burials in the cemetery, including 11 Canadians. St. Omer was a major aerodrome for the Luftwaffe during the Battle of Britain and subsequent air operations. South-west of St. Omer (Wizernes) are the German buzz-bomb (V-1s) runways. The Doodlebugs were sent over England from June until September 1944, when the runways were captured by the First Canadian Army.

Etaples Military Cemetery

Etaples cemetery is on the coastal road between Boulogne and Le Touquet, three km north of Etaples (100 km west of Arras). Etaples was the major depot base for the British army on the Western Front and was the location of the infamous Bull Ring and the British mutiny in 1917. The cemetery was used by Hospitals throughout the war and contains 10,729 Commonwealth soldiers, including 1,123 Canadians. It is the second largest Commonwealth cemetery in France, only St.Sever Communal Cemetery & Extension in Rouen is larger.

This cemetery reflects the Canadian losses in the major actions of the Somme, Vimy, Passchendaele and the Advance to Victory. There are 149 Canadian Somme burials here.

On May 19th, 1918, German Gotha bombers bombed the depots and direct hits were received on the No.1 Canadian General hospital, killing 66, including three Canadian Nursing Sisters. The men killed in the attack are buried in Plots LXV to LXVIII. The Officers and Nursing Sisters are buried in Plot XXVIII.

The grave of Lieutenant F.W. Campbell, VC in Boulogne Eastern Cemetery. (Christie)

There are 119 second World War burials in the cemetery, including five Canadians.

Boulogne Eastern Cemetery

Boulogne is 100 km west of Arras on the English Channel coast. The cemetery, in the eastern part of the city, was used from 1914 to 1918 and contains 442 Canadian burials. Due to soil conditions, the headstones lie flat. A hospital centre throughout the war, Boulogne is typical of many hospital centre cemeteries. The officers are separated from the other ranks, the men are buried in chronological order, three to a grave here, and there are few unknowns.

The Canadians buried here died of wounds received in every Canadian action from 1915-1917. There are fifty men buried here who died of wounds received in the Second Battle of Ypres, 1915, 57 from the Battle of the Somme, 54 from Mount Sorrel and 109 who died as a result of wounds received in the Battle of Vimy Ridge.

Of interest is the grave of Lieutenant Frederick W. Campbell, VC, of the 1st Canadian Battalion (Western Ontario). Campbell won his Victoria Cross for bravery in the Battle of Givenchy in June 1915. He was severely wounded in the action and died four days later.

Alwyn Bramley-Moore, Princess Patricia's Canadian Light Infantry, is buried in Plot VIII, Row D, Grave 91. A transplanted Englishman, Bramley-Moore wrote of his wartime life in letters to his family, later published in a book entitled *The Path Of Duty*. His war was cut short when he was mortally wounded by a sniper on the Ypres front, March 28th, 1916. He died on April 4th.

The cemetery also contains 224 graves from the Second World War, including 18 Canadians, and a plot of Portuguese burials from the First World War.

For Further Reference

This guide has focussed solely on the actions of Canadian troops in the Battles of Festubert and Givenchy, 1915, and the Battle of Hill 70, 1917. However, fighting along the Western Front was continuous throughout the war and hundreds of thousands were killed there. This was the heart of the Great War and today the monuments and cemeteries of the British, French, Belgians, Germans, Australians and New Zealanders are densely scattered throughout the region. There are many good books that allow us to revisit this past era, and it is difficult not to feel the sorrow of those times. Below are listed a few titles to help those who wish to make a Pilgrimage to the Western Front.

Before Endeavours Fade, by the late Rose Coombs (the best guide book on the Western Front), Battle of Britain Prints, 1976.
Australian Battlefields of the Western Front 1916-18, by John Laffin, Kangaroo Press, 1992.
Thirteen Years After by W.R. Bird. CEF Books, 2001.
For King & Empire; The Canadians in the Great War, Vols I-X by N.M. Christie, CEF Books, 1996-2007.
The Great War As I Saw It by F.G. Scott. CEF Books, 2000.
Silhouettes of The Great War by J.H. Becker. CEF Books, 2001.
The 50th Battalion in No Man's Land by V. Wheeler. CEF Books.

Books that pertain to the Battles of Festubert and Givenchy are few, but those dedicated to the Battle of Hill 70, 1917 are nonexistent. The books listed below are the best.

Canada in Flanders Volumes I, II by Lord Beaverbrook. Hodder and Stoughton, 1916, 1917.
The Official History of the Canadian Expeditionary Force 1914-19 by G.W.L. Nicholson, The Queen's Printer, 1962.
The Journal of Private Fraser edited by R.H. Roy. CEF Books 1998
Letters of Agar Adamson edited by N.M. Christie. CEF Books 1997.
The Donkeys by Alan Clarke. Hutchinson, 1961.
1915 by Lyn McDonald. Headline, 1993.
The Indian Corps in France by J.W. Merrewether, John Murray, 1917.
Sepoys in the Trenches by G. Corrigan. Spellmount, 1988.

Sentimental Sheet Music was very popular during the Great War. Both Composers, Bruno and Rose, fought at Festubert.